TL;DR: FINANCIAL LITERACY EMPLOYEES IN THE WYOMING PUBLIC EMPLOYEE PENSION PLAN

Optimizing Financial Decisions Based On Your Wyoming Retirement System Benefits

Karl Fisch
Jill Thompson

D1253645

CONTENTS

TL;DR: internet abbreviation for "too long, didn't read," meaning a post, article, or anything with words was too long, and whoever used the phrase didn't read it for that reason (source: Urban Dictionary). Each section of this book will include a brief TL;DR summary at the beginning of the section.

"Luck is what happens when preparation meets opportunity." — Seneca

Visit **fischlearning.com/tldr-wyoming** for links to websites, blogs, books, spreadsheets and other resources to learn more about all the topics covered in this book. If you have questions or feedback, or simply want to talk about your financial situation, please reach out to me at **karl@fischlearning.com**.

Other Books by Karl
Find the entire TL;DR: Financial Literacy
Series at **http://bit.ly/fischtldr**

For my wife
The best teacher I've ever met.
And my best friend.

For my husband
The man who has always been by my side living the good life!

How This Book Is Organized

This book is divided into four major sections.

Part 1: Financial Literacy Basics for Everyone
Part 1 covers the information about financial literacy that is applicable to everyone, not just WRS members. Note that this part stands on its own and does not assume you are a WRS member.

Part 2: Your WRS Benefits
Part 2 focuses on your WRS benefits along with other benefits from your school district.

Part 3: How to Optimize Your Financial Planning to Take Advantage of Your WRS Benefits
Part 3 focuses on how you can optimize the decisions described in Part 1 based on your WRS benefits described in Part 2.

Part 4: Scenario Planning
Part 4 looks at several different "life scenarios" for WRS members as examples of how you might combine Parts 1 through 3 into a coherent retirement plan.

Conclusion
Some closing thoughts, a request for feedback, and links to further resources.

Important: Both tax laws (frequently) and WRS benefit rules (occasionally) can change over time. As they change after publication of this book, we will do our best to keep the book updated. If you purchased the digital version, we will update it at Amazon and you can download the new version. If you purchased the print edition - or if you don't want to reread the entire digital version just to see what's changed - we will summarize the updates at **fischlearning.com/tldr-wyoming**.

PART 1: FINANCIAL LITERACY BASICS FOR EVERYONE

Part 1 covers the information about financial literacy that is applicable to everyone, not just WRS members. Note that this part stands on its own and does not assume you are a WRS member.

1.1: INTRO & PURPOSE

TL;DR: Finances are such a huge part of your life that you should take the time to thoroughly educate yourself. Since many folks won't do that, this book is an attempt to quickly give you the basics. Many Wyoming educators are also unaware of the fantastic advantages their WRS benefits give them and how those should impact many of their other financial decisions.

You shouldn't read this book. Really, you shouldn't. It's not that it's a bad book, it's just that it's an overly simplified look at finances and the decisions everyone should make to have a secure life financially. There are so many really good and much more in-depth resources that are readily available, both in books and on websites, that you should take advantage of those and give yourself the financial education you deserve. It wouldn't take a huge amount of time, perhaps somewhere between twenty and thirty hours to get a good grounding, and maybe between fifty and one hundred to be very well versed in almost everything you need to know. That may sound like a lot, but in comparison to the over 700,000 hours (and maybe many more) you are likely to be alive, it's a very small investment (pun intended). And since finances are such a huge part of your life, and of living your life the way you want to live it, it's worth the time investment. Compared to the over 14,000 hours you likely spent learning in K-12 schools (plus any post-secondary education), isn't it worth twenty to one hundred more to educate yourself in order to make good financial decisions?

"How long are you going to wait before you demand the best for yourself?" – *Epictetus*

But many folks won't. There are a variety of reasons people don't invest the time to learn about finances.

- I'm really busy and it would take too long

- I wouldn't understand it anyway (I'm not smart enough/I'm not good at math)

- It doesn't matter because I don't make that much money and financial planning is for rich people

- The culture (at least in the United States) is that we don't talk about money and our finances

Or you may have a completely different reason. Whatever the reason, most people we know tend to move through their financial lives day by day, week by week, month by month, paycheck by paycheck. It's not that they don't try to make good financial decisions, or that they never plan ahead financially, it's that they don't take the time and make the effort to make a **coherent plan** for how they want to lead their financial lives. And they don't realize how simple most of the financial decisions they need to make are, and how easy it is to make good ones.

So this book is for those folks; for those people who won't take twenty (or thirty or fifty or one hundred) hours to really educate themselves, but can convince themselves to take one or two hours. By necessity, this will be a simplified look at finances and financial decisions for Wyoming educators who are WRS members. (Most Wyoming educators are not fully aware of their WRS benefits and how that should impact many of their other financial decisions throughout their adult lives.) We won't thoroughly explain topics. We won't discuss and link to the research that backs up the assertions. We won't have a lot of charts and tables, personal vignettes, or worksheets for you to complete. We will simply give advice that will be appropriate to about 90% of people about 90% of the time. (We completely made those percentages up, but estimate they are likely within ±5%.)

Most of the financial decisions we need to make in our lives are really relatively straightforward, and it doesn't take much more than an hour or two to go over them in a (superficial) fashion. Personal Finance is just that, it's "personal," so no book or website is going to be able to give you everything you need to know that is perfect for your individual circumstances. The hope is that perhaps, after reading this book (if you do), you will have the interest and the confidence to perhaps invest a few more hours to more thoroughly educate yourself, and to fill in the gaps in your "personal" situation that this book didn't adequately address. We could say a lot more but, well, that would kind of defeat the whole purpose of this book. If this book ends up too long and you don't read it, then we've failed (hence, the TL;DR).

Before we go any further, some disclosures, with Karl going first. I am not a financial planner. I have no formal training in personal finance or investing, and no certifications. I am simply a lifelong learner, constantly curious, and have been interested in personal finance since working in a credit union during high school and college. I have continued to learn about finances my entire adult life and have frequently served as a resource for friends, family and colleagues. I somehow became the "go to" guy in my high school for other educators who had questions about school district benefits, Colorado PERA (Colorado's pension plan), and just finances in general. Partially as a result of that experience, I see the necessity for a book such as this, so I wanted to do my part to try to help educators become financially literate and optimize their financial lives based on their pension benefits. While it would be nice to make a little bit of money from this, that's not really my expectation or my goal. This is a passion project for me.

I hope you find it helpful.

Jill, here. Like Karl, I am not a financial planner nor did I study finance in college. When I began teaching, I knew nothing about retirement planning and assumed the pension my husband and I would receive after teaching in the state of Iowa would take care of us. Just 10 years into our teaching careers; however, we moved to Wyoming and "started over." During the two decades I've taught in Wyoming, spreading personal finance knowledge has become my passion not only to the ~120 students I teach each year, but also to the adults I work with and also come into contact with. As I inch my way closer to retirement, my goal is to help all WRS members to gain more knowledge at an earlier age. I must thank Tim Ranzetta and Jessica Endlich, co-founders of NextGen Personal Finance, who have an endless passion for helping students and teachers alike with improving their financial literacy awareness.

So, about 100 pages. About an hour or two. Let's get started.

1.2: PHILOSOPHY & LIVING THE GOOD LIFE

TL;DR: Financial planning should enable you to live the life you want to live.

We almost left this section out, because it's more "explanation" and we're trying to avoid that and just get to the nitty gritty details (and hope that you will continue your education to learn more). But, in the end, we decided it was important to devote at least a short section to the purpose of financial planning (or at least our take on it). It provides a needed conceptual framework for how to think about the decisions discussed in the rest of the book, so bear with us for a few paragraphs.

Some people view financial planning as a way to get rich, others as a way to get by, and still others as a way to not just get by, but to be "secure" - whatever that means to them. Here is how we view financial planning: it's a necessary and critical part of living the good life. What's a "good life"? We don't know, everyone's definition is different. What's important is that you take the time to define what a good life is for you, and then **align your financial decisions with your values**.

"First say to yourself what you would be; and then do what you have to do." – Epictetus

All the "conventional wisdom," all the "rules of thumb" that are talked about in financial circles (and we will include a few ourselves), assume that your vision of a good life is the same as whomever is telling you about the rule of thumb. While sometimes that will be a good fit, often it won't, and that's why it's really important to define what a "good life" looks like to you before embarking on this process. The key is making your own decisions in such a way that you are most likely to attain your version of the good life. The goal of this book is to help you plan your finances in such a way that you have the independence to lead the life you want to live; to give you as much control as possible over your financial situation so that your finances don't prevent you from living the life you want.

It's really that simple.

1.3: BASIC EQUATION: INCOME - EXPENSES = SAVINGS + INVESTMENTS

***TL;DR**: Make a budget if you wish, but it's more helpful to proactively focus on the four components of the equation.*

Karl loves math. Karl taught teenagers mathematics for his entire adult life. But we're going to try to keep the math in this book to a minimum. It's not that we think you can't understand it (people aren't "bad" at math, they were often just bad at doing math class in school), it's that it's too easy to get distracted by the math (and miss the forest for the trees). But there's one basic equation that is important enough to include:

Income - Expenses = Savings + Investments

That equation really defines the parameters for every financial discussion/decision in this book. You start with your income, how much you make from your job(s) and any other sources of income you might have. Then you subtract off your expenses, what you spend. Whatever is left (and it's critical that there is something left) you can then decide to divide up between savings (money you might need in the relatively short term) and investments (money you won't need in the short term and therefore want to invest so that it will grow over time).

This is typically the point in a financial book where it would talk about the importance of a budget. We're not going to do that. If you want to learn more about budgets, there are lots of books and websites that will help you and, for some folks, that might even be helpful. But in our experience, focusing on making a budget is an approach that isn't very helpful for most people. The way most people make budgets is **reactive**, they let their current circumstances define their budget and then point to the realities of the budget as the reason they can't get ahead. For most people, we think it's more helpful to be **proactive**, to recognize the realities (you do have to eat) but to design the life you want to lead instead of being restricted by the "assumed" realities of your current circumstances.

So, we're not going to specifically work on a budget in this book. Instead, we'll focus on the four components of that equation: **Income**, **expenses**, **savings**, and **investments**.

Income is how much you make, typically from your job(s), but some people have other sources of income as well. Obviously the larger your income is, the more money you have to work with, so if you have some ways to increase that income without negatively affecting your lifestyle (the good life, however you define that), do that. This can include doing things at your current job to increase your income, like taking on more responsibility, working more hours or a different shift, or increasing your skills in a way that makes you more valuable. It could also include other ways of making income, often referred to as "side hustles," things you do outside your regular job to earn extra income. It's really important that if you decide to take on any side hustles that you only take on those that provide some extra income but don't negatively affect the life you want to live.

> *"What difference does it make, after all, what your position in life is if you dislike it yourself?"* – *Seneca*

And, ultimately, it will be **passive income**, income you make from your investments, that will allow you to retire.

Expenses are what you spend your money on, and this is the component that you typically have the most control over (see the next chapter). This will require the most thinking and work on your part to align your expenses with the life you want to live.

Savings is the money you have set aside for possible short-term use. It's money that you don't need to live on day-to-day or week-to-week, but that is available either for some expense you know is coming up (maybe holiday presents you are planning on buying, or perhaps you know you will be buying a new computer in the next year), or as a "rainy day" fund for an unexpected expense (your water heater needs service).

Investments is the money you have set aside for the long-term and, next to expenses, is the component you will want to do the most thinking about. Some people have trouble distinguishing between savings and investments, it's really the factors of time and purpose that distinguish them. Savings is short-term and its purpose is much more limited. Investments are long-term - we're going to say money you don't plan on spending for at least five years (and hopefully many more) - and the purpose is typically (although not always) broader.

So, that's enough explanation, let's dive in.

1.4: SPENDING & SAVING

TL; DR: Your savings rate is more important than how much you earn on investments. And since your spending determines your savings rate, your spending rate is key.

"Curb your desire—don't set your heart on so many things and you will get what you need." – Epictetus

A lot of people spend a lot of time talking about how to make a lot of money in the stock market. We'll certainly spend a little time later in this book on the topic of investments as well. But a key point to remember is that you can't control what the market returns, the market is going to do its thing no matter what you do. What you can control is how much you save and therefore how much you invest. Your savings rate is much more important than trying to beat the market with your investments.

And here's the thing, your savings rate is really just a reflection of your spending. While there are certainly things you can do to increase your income, on a day-to-day basis most people have much more discretion over what they spend than over what they make. So your savings rate is pretty much going to be determined by your spending; spend less, save more (and then invest more). (See **bit.ly/spendingmatters** and **bit.ly/tldrpenny** for more.)

There have been entire books written about this, but this is the Karl-and-Jill's Notes version (sorry Cliff and Spark):

- In general, spending on "things" doesn't bring you

happiness. Spending on experiences that are meaningful to you is more likely to increase your happiness.

● Human beings adjust quickly to new circumstances. In terms of spending, this is often referred to as the "**hedonic treadmill.**" When you buy something new, you experience pleasure for a little while, then you get used to it and you need to buy something else to get a new fix. As your income (hopefully) increases over time, so does your lifestyle, so things that used to be "luxuries" are now considered necessities, and you begin inflating your lifestyle to match your new earnings (this is often referred to as "**lifestyle creep**"). Once you get on this "hedonic treadmill," it's hard to get off.

● "Keeping up with the Joneses" is a cliche, but it's a cliche that is based in truth. The problem is that your neighbors' (or friends', or family's) spending is visible, but their savings isn't. When your next door neighbor gets a new car, you'll probably see it. When your next door neighbor contributes more to their 401k, IRA or 403b, you probably won't.

● "**Opportunity Cost**" is an economic term, but it's pretty easy to understand. If you spend money (or time) on one thing, you don't have that money (or time) available to spend on something else. Every time you buy something, ask yourself if six months later you'll look at that purchase and it will make you happy. Or go through your credit card statement line by line and ask the same thing. Remind yourself every time you are about to buy something, what else you could spend that money on, the opportunity cost, and then make the decision that will make you the happiest. This doesn't mean you can't ever buy stuff, but it means you need to be **intentional** about it. Every **$100 in spending per month that you can cut** out will turn into **$150,000 thirty years from now** (assuming you invest the $100 every month and earn 8% annual return). **That's** opportunity cost.

- Be more explicit with your goals. Instead of saying, "I want to save more," say "I want to save x% of my income so that we can buy a house in three years."

Again, this could go on for a while, but we'll cut it short. A lot of folks want to know how much they should save. 10% of what they make? 15%? For us, that's the wrong way to go about it. You should figure out what makes you happy, what kind of life you want to live, what your goals are, and then act (and spend, and save) accordingly.

We will say that for anyone making a middle class or better income, we think saving 10% is way too low. Most of us managed to live on less than 50% of what we're making now (in college, or when we first moved out on our own), and life was still pretty good. Get off of the hedonic treadmill, avoid lifestyle creep, and make intentional choices and you'll find that you can save much more than you thought possible. While intentional spending in every area is important, housing, transportation and food are the "big rocks" that make the most difference, and we'll talk about those a bit later.

Next we'll talk about some of the specific financial "infrastructure" decisions you might want to make.

1.5: BANK ACCOUNTS

TL;DR: You need a checking and a savings account. You should not be paying any fees for just having those accounts, and they should be earning competitive interest.

"You're better off not giving the small things more time than they deserve." – Marcus Aurelius

Most people need two - and only two - accounts at their bank or credit union. A checking account and a savings account. There are lots of good choices of banks or credit unions depending on where you live and where you work, but here are the non-negotiables:

• Your checking account needs to be **free**. No fees just for having the account open, and no minimum balance. It's okay if it requires a direct deposit, because you should be having your paycheck direct-deposited into the account. Ideally, your checking account would even earn a little interest.

• Your savings account also needs to be free, with no fees and no minimum balance. It should earn interest, and the amount of interest it earns should be competitive with the other choices out there.

If you're not sure if your current accounts meet these criteria, look into it. As of this writing, a good bank to compare to is Ally Bank (**ally.com**). Compare your current accounts to Ally's checking and savings accounts (which have no fees and both pay interest), including the interest they are earning. If there is a significant difference, or if there are fees attached to your current accounts, switch. Note that it doesn't have to be Ally, that's just a good comparison as of this writing.

1.6: CREDIT CARDS & LOANS

TL;DR: Credit cards can be the downfall or a way to enhance your finances. It all depends on how you use them.

"What lies in our power to do, lies in our power not to do."
— Aristotle

Used poorly, credit cards get a lot of folks in trouble. Used well, credit cards can be a valuable way to not only track and manage your spending, but to actually increase your savings. You know yourself better than anyone, so figure out whether you can be the type of person that uses them well, or not. If not, then it's probably best not to have one (or perhaps to have one for emergencies that you don't carry with you) and only use cash, checks and debit cards. Set up the credit card so that the full balance is paid automatically from your checking account each month, no matter what, and then go on with your life.

If you're disciplined enough to use credit cards well, then take advantage of them. There are many credit cards that actually pay you to use them, through signup bonuses and cash back offers. The reason they do this, of course, is to take advantage of folks who will then spend more and/or not pay off their balances each month and therefore pay interest, so you only want to take advantage of these offers if that won't be you.

There are many websites you can visit to compare current credit card offers (see **fischlearning.com/tldr-wyoming** for links) but, in general, pick the cards that offer you rewards in the categories that best match your spending, and the ones that offer you cash back as opposed to points to be used toward other purchases. For example, most people spend (or at least they should spend) a significant portion of their income on groceries, so having a credit card that gives you extra cash back at the grocery store you frequent is an obvious choice.

> **Note**: There are some people who use credit cards well for travel hacking where you will want to accumulate points and spend them later on travel - if you spend a lot on traveling, you might go in this direction instead of cash back.

If you're disciplined, there's no reason you can't have multiple cards that offer rewards in different categories and simply use the appropriate card in the appropriate places (or have certain bills automatically charged to the credit card that has the higher reward for that category). Stagger when you get the cards so you can take advantage of the signup bonuses (typically requires a minimum spend in a certain amount of time), and keep an eye on your credit score so you don't open up too many, too fast. But as long as you set them all to pay off automatically each month, having multiple credit cards can actually increase your credit score because part of the calculation for your score is the amount of available credit you are using. See **bit.ly/tldrcc1** and **bit.ly/ tldrcc2** for more.)

Credit cards are also helpful as a way to keep track of your spending, so you can identify areas where you are perhaps spending more than you thought. It's easy when spending cash, or even using a debit card, to not notice how much you are spending on Starbucks (as just one example, not trying to pick on Starbucks). But if you use a credit card, and then take a moment to examine your statement each month, you'll get a better idea of what you are actually spending money on. You can even use free tools like **Personal Capital (personalcapital.com)** that you can set up to automatically bring in your accounts and it will keep track for you. Review the categories in light of opportunity costs and your definition of the good life, and go from there.

A brief note about loans: try to avoid them. In a tl;dr book, we can't go into the complexities of loans but, much like with the discussion of spending and the use of credit cards above, if you live within (hopefully well within) your means, you shouldn't have to resort to getting a loan very often (if at all).

Obviously, if you choose to buy a house, the vast majority of folks will have to take out a mortgage. If owning a home is part of the life you want to live, then that would be a "good" loan to get. (In general, for mortgages you want to get the lowest fixed rate mortgage you can.) Lots of folks think a car loan is a necessity but, as discussed in the next section, it might not be. If you have to have a car and can't afford to pay cash for it, then buy a reliable, used car, pay as much cash as you can, then get a loan for the rest that you pay off as quickly as possible. Once you have that first car you should be able to avoid loans for any future car purchases.

1.7: HOUSING, TRANSPORTATION & FOOD

TL;DR: Conventional wisdom on where to live, what to live in, what to drive, and where and what to eat is often wrong, or at least not thoughtful and intentional enough. Take some time to match your choices with your definition of the good life.

"It is not that we have so little time but that we lose so much." — Seneca

Conventional wisdom...

- "Buy a house as soon as you can."

- "Buy as big of a house as you can afford."

- "Move-up to a bigger, nicer house as soon as you can afford to."

- "Buy a nice car that holds its value and makes your commute as enjoyable as possible."

- "We 'deserve' to eat out."

All of these statements might fall under "conventional wisdom," and all of them are wrong for a significant number of people. To be clear, **they may not be wrong for you**, but housing, transportation and food are three of the biggest and most consequential financial decisions you make in your life and they have an outsized effect on the quality of your life, so it's important to get these right.

Like all other financial decisions, you should make these in the context of the good life you want to live and what truly makes you happy. The so-called "American Dream" tends to include owning your own (large) house with a nice lawn, and several late-model cars in the driveway, that you use to take you to restaurants to eat out frequently. If that's truly what you want, there's nothing wrong with that. But, for many (perhaps most) folks, those decisions are often made on autopilot and don't actually align with their version of the good life.

Some things for you to consider and research more:

- For a lot of folks, home ownership is actually less convenient, more restrictive, and more expensive than renting. The conventional wisdom that renting is throwing your money away while owning is investing can be correct, but often is not. And when you add in the time and hassle requirements of owning a home, along with the opportunity cost, renting is often the better choice.

- If you do decide to buy a house, try to "right-size" it the first time. Every time you "move-up" to a new house, the transaction costs can be expensive, not to mention the increased time and spending associated with moving. That doesn't necessarily mean "buy the biggest house you can afford," it means trying to figure out what size house you will need for the size of family you'll have, and then waiting to purchase until you can afford that house. A good rule of thumb would be to put at least 20% down and make sure your payments will last for no more than 15 years, and will be less than 25% of your take home pay (although not everyone chooses to do this).

- Research consistently shows that commute times are negatively correlated with and are one of the biggest impediments to happiness. The longer the commute, the less happy people are. This is a huge issue that most folks don't think about when choosing where to live. Yes, folks will look for a house within a reasonable commute of their work, but give some more thought to what "reasonable" really is. And if you can, live close enough to work that you don't need to use a car at all (walk, bike, or use public transportation - it will not only save you a ton of money, it will improve your health).

• In addition to robbing you of happiness, commutes are expensive. Don't assume you have to own a car, or multiple cars. Think carefully about where you are going to live in relation to where you work. This one decision - finding a place to live near where you work - can be **the** deciding factor in your financial success. Most folks have no idea how much they truly spend on their cars over their lifetime. Eliminating or reducing this increases happiness and financial well-being.

• If you do end up buying a car (or two or three), think carefully about what you need. In the United States, SUV's and heavy-duty pickup trucks are really, really popular. But most people don't need those capabilities for their daily commute, only for occasional use. (Pro-tip: two parents and up to three kids can truly fit in a typical sedan - depending on their respective ages and number of car seats you need at any one time.) Consider purchasing a more economical vehicle (both in terms of purchase price and operating costs) and, on the occasions when you need the SUV or pickup, rent one. (Or if you own multiple vehicles, have one efficient one and one more heavy-duty). You'll come out way ahead in the end. (Of course, in Wyoming there are definitely cases where an SUV or heavy-duty pickup is essential.) And, as we write this, buying an electric vehicle is probably the best choice not only for the environment, but for your finances, as they have a much lower total cost of ownership.

• One place where conventional wisdom is usually correct

is buying used vehicles versus new. The quality of cars has increased dramatically in the last 20 years, so buying a three, five, or eight-year-old car is not that risky these days, and can save you a lot of money. This is especially helpful if you are also making choices that minimize how much you have to use the car, as that will increase its effective lifespan. Buy used, buy economical, drive less, and keep for as long as it runs will have huge positive effects on your finances and your happiness.

- Think carefully about food and the value (to you) of eating out. While there's nothing wrong with eating out occasionally, it is incredibly more expensive than eating at home. Many Americans have gotten in the habit of eating as many meals (or more) out as they do at home, and that's had disastrous effects on their finances. Evaluate whether what you really value is eating the food at the restaurant, or eating good food with family and good friends. If it's the latter, you can almost certainly spend much less money, eat just as well, and actually have a better time at home.

Don't assume you have to buy a house or a car, and don't assume you have to go out to eat to have a good time. If you do, don't assume you have to spend as much on those things as others think you do. And pay very careful attention to the location of where you live compared to where you work. It's important enough that you should consider changing either where you live or where you work to minimize your commute and your expenses. It's truly that important.

1.8: INSURANCE

TL;DR: The purpose of insurance is to protect you against large expenses, not to "pay for stuff." Buy the least expensive insurance that adequately accomplishes that task.

"We should always be asking ourselves: 'Is this something that is, or is not, in my control?'" —Epictetus

Many folks in Jill and Karl's generations grew up with the idea that insurance was supposed to pay for things. Particularly when it came to medical insurance, the feeling was that insurance should pay for everything - or almost everything - and we (individuals) should pay very little. Setting aside any political viewpoints, under our current system this just isn't possible.

Insurance companies have to make enough money to cover expenses (which includes any claims you make plus the overhead of administering the program) and, if they are for-profit, have to make a profit above and beyond that. The only way to do that is to make sure the combination of the premiums you pay plus any out-of-pocket expenses you pay adds up to at least what their expenses are plus whatever profit they make. Your employer likely covers at least some of your premium (for health, dental and perhaps vision insurance), but you have to pay the rest. Most employers offer at least some choice of plans, with the differences between the plans mostly a tradeoff between a higher premium with lower out-of-pocket expenses or a lower premium with higher out-of-pocket expenses.

Every individual's situation is unique, of course, but generally you want to purchase the least expensive insurance that protects you from **catastrophic** expenses. That's the original idea behind insurance, that a group of people pool their money so that when something unfortunate happens to one person, their life isn't ruined. For that to happen; however, there have to be other people who end up paying **more** for insurance than for the benefit they actually receive. Instead of looking at insurance as "paying for things," try to reframe your thinking to insurance as "protecting against catastrophe." You are going to need to pay for the things you use, insurance is there for the hopefully uncommon occurrence of massive expenses (your house burns down, you have a major medical condition, etc.).

If you make your insurance choices with that mindset, you will most likely choose to increase your deductibles (whether that be for car, house or medical) in exchange for lower premiums. That still provides you the security that if something tragic and expensive occurs, it won't bankrupt you, while paying for the services you use. It will also likely lower your premiums for insurance, which provides you extra cash along the way, but it's really important to set aside that cash to cover the increased out-of-pocket expenses you may have. (If you have a high-deductible health plan, for example, we would highly recommend you put any premium savings into an HSA, which is discussed later.)

Life insurance is a bit too complicated to cover in a tl;dr book, but a few quick thoughts. In general, if you have people who are dependent on your income (typically kids, sometimes a spouse), you will want to have life insurance to make up for your lost income should you die earlier than expected. Our suggestion for most people's situation is to purchase low-cost, term life insurance. Typically that means you would have a fixed premium for the term of the policy, and you would select the term based on how long you needed to replace your income. That often (but not always) means a 20-year term, as that gets your kids to the age where they are independent (or hopefully at least close to independent) and won't need your income. Keep in mind that you often have a certain amount of life insurance paid by your employer and you may receive a death benefit from TRS, so factor those amounts in as well. How much to purchase is a personal decision and should be reevaluated periodically. Be sure to get quotes from multiple companies. At that time of this writing, **policygenius.com** is a great website to get quotes from multiple agencies.

> **Note**: It's also really important that you have designated beneficiaries on all of your accounts (bank, brokerage, retirement, TRS, etc.) to make sure your wishes are followed should you pass away, and to make things much easier for your beneficiaries. Everyone should also have at least a will, power of attorney, and health care directive. Unless you have a complicated situation, you can create these for free at **freewill.com** (or, of course, you can work with an attorney).

So, consider raising the deductible on your auto and home/renters insurance. Consider a high-deductible health care plan and put the premium savings into an HSA (and invest them). And, perhaps most importantly, try to live your life in a way that decreases the risks that you have a large claim. Drive responsibly, wear your seatbelt, eat right and exercise. All of those things will not only make your life better, but make it much more likely you won't have to pay those out-of-pocket expenses to reach your deductible.

1.9: TAXES

TL;DR: For most people, taxes aren't very complicated. There are some simple things you can do to minimize the taxes you pay but, for the most part, don't spend a lot of time thinking (or worrying) about taxes.

"In America, there are two tax systems; one for the informed and one for the uninformed. Both systems are legal." —Judge Learned Hand

For the majority of folks, taxes should be pretty simple these days. You're most likely going to take the standard deduction at the federal level, so the only things to think about are ways to minimize your taxable income and occasionally to take advantage of special tax incentives (e.g., **Savers Credit**, or the tax credit for purchasing an electric vehicle). Even if you do have enough deductions to itemize, it's probably worth more of your time to think about minimizing your taxable income.

Obviously in a book like this we're not going to cover all the ins-and-outs of the tax code, but let's just hit the highlights of what you want to consider. For most people, the main ways to minimize your taxable income is to contribute to a 401k/403b/457/ IRA/FSA/Dependent Care Spending Account/etc., make sure any health insurance premiums you pay through your employer come out pre-tax and, if you have a high-deductible health care plan, contribute as much as you can to your HSA.

We'll talk more about tax-advantaged savings plans below but, for the purposes of this section, here's what you need to know. Any money you contribute to a Traditional 401k/403b/457/IRA plan comes out pre-tax, which means you won't have to pay any federal or state income taxes on that money in the year that you earn it. (Keep in mind you will end up eventually paying taxes when you withdraw it, hopefully many years in the future during retirement). So, for example, if you are in the 22% federal tax bracket, for every $100 you contribute to your Traditional 401k/403b/457/IRA plan, your net paycheck will only go down by $78 (because you won't be withholding/paying $22 in taxes to the U.S. government).

But in many states, it gets even better, because they likely also give you a tax break. So depending on what tax bracket you are in for your state, your net paycheck will go down even less. For example, Colorado has a flat tax of 4.55%. So, for every $100 you contribute your net paycheck will only go down by $73.45. (Obviously, **this doesn't apply in Wyoming** since you don't have a state income tax.) Note that if you are part of a pension plan, 401k/403b/457 contributions typically do not reduce your pension contribution, but your pension contribution itself comes out before federal and state taxes are assessed (similar to Social Security contributions).

Many employers also offer a Roth version of 401k/403b/457 plans, plus you can invest in a Roth IRA outside of your employer. These dollars are post-tax, meaning you don't get a tax break now, but any earnings and future withdrawals are tax free. Depending on your income, current tax bracket, expected pension or social security benefits, and future tax rates, it may make sense to split your money between the Traditional (pre-tax) and Roth (post-tax) plans.

In addition to any contributions you make to a retirement plan, most employers allow you to choose to pay insurance premiums with pre-tax money (referred to as **Section 125 plans**). Very few people should choose not to take advantage of this, so check your pay stub or with your Human Resources department to make sure you are. You can also have money for child care expenses and flexible spending accounts pulled out pre-tax, and you should definitely take advantage of those when you can. (One notable exception: for some pension plans you may want to stop paying premiums and having other deductions come out pre-tax during your last years of service in order to maximize your pension benefit.)

Finally, if you have a high-deductible health care plan, you will want to take advantage of **Health Savings Accounts** (HSAs). These are known as "triple-tax-advantaged" plans, because not only are your contributions pre-tax, but your savings can be invested and grown tax free, and then your withdrawals are also tax free if used for medical expenses. In other words, you **never** pay tax on this money. Often employers will contribute a small amount to your HSA, but you can also choose to contribute out of your paycheck. The more you contribute (within the federal limit), the lower your taxes will be.

> **Note**: Remember, **HSA** accounts values carry over at the end of the calendar year, but money left in **FSA** accounts is surrendered. Make sure you are clear which you are funding.

Not only will you pay less in taxes if you lower your taxable income, but lowering your taxable income often allows you to qualify for more tax credits, which lowers the taxes you have to pay even more. Many tax credits (incentives) have an income limit where they get phased out and, for some of them, all of the above pre-tax contributions are taken into account when calculating that limit. So by lowering your taxable income, you just might qualify for more tax credits (the Savers Credit is a good one to look at, particularly at the beginning of your career when you are not making as much).

> **Quick reminder**: The information in this book is not a substitute for contacting a tax professional. Please contact a tax professional to clarify and confirm your plan before acting!

1.10: INVESTING: ASSET ALLOCATION

TL;DR: Next to the amount you save, the most important part of investing isn't choosing the individual investments, it's choosing your asset allocation. How you divide up your investments among different types of assets (stocks, bonds, etc.) is the main determiner of your investment returns.

"The fox knows many things, but the hedgehog knows one big thing." — Archilochus

Choosing investments freaks people out. There is so much information out there that it can be overwhelming and, because they fear making a "mistake," many people end up making poor investment decisions by not making any investment decisions. The good news is that it really isn't that difficult, you just have to make a few pretty simple decisions and perhaps make some small adjustments over time. That's it.

One can devise a really complicated investment strategy, using lots of different asset classes and lots of exotic products, but those complicated investment strategies rarely (if ever) pay off. In fact, the vast majority of investors will earn better investment returns by sticking with a simple, low-cost asset allocation consisting of stocks and bonds. If you really get into investing and want to tweak your portfolio and invest in additional asset classes, you can maybe squeeze a little bit more return over time, but you're also just as likely (probably more likely) to underperform.

So here's what 95% of investors should do. Save as much as you can and invest it in perhaps three different "buckets": a **short-term bucket**, a **medium-term bucket**, and a **long-term bucket**.

As always, individual circumstances vary but, in general, any money that you think you might want to spend in the next five or so years you should consider a short-term investment (really more savings than investment), in five to fifteen years a medium-term investment, and all other investment money (typically retirement) consider a long-term investment. Your asset allocation for each bucket will be different, with the short-term bucket invested much more conservatively and your long-term bucket invested much more aggressively, and the medium-term in between. (Don't let the choice of the term "aggressive" frighten you, it simply means that since you are investing for the long-term, you can tolerate any short-term drop in the markets.)

How you divide up your investments in each bucket depends on your tolerance for risk. This is really mostly looking at the risk of *your own behavior* undermining your investment returns. If you invest more "aggressively" and the markets go down, will you freak out and sell (and therefore be "buying high and selling low")? If so, then you might set your asset allocation more conservatively. If you understand how markets work long term, and therefore control your own behavior, you can invest more "aggressively" and therefore earn a higher return over time. (Again, investing "aggressively" doesn't mean you're being unduly risky, it just means you are investing in assets that will have a better return over the long-term, with the chance that they will be more volatile in the short-term.)

So, what does this look like? Again, individual circumstances matter, but here's a good place to start. Your short-term bucket is money you plan on spending in the next five years or so. A common example of this is saving for a down-payment on a house (or perhaps to buy a car). Because stocks can go down and stay down for a while, you generally don't want very much of this money invested in stocks. So your short-term bucket should be invested primarily in bonds, perhaps certificates of deposits, and your savings account. You may want to have a relatively small percentage invested in stocks as well (see the next section for more on this).

For your medium-term bucket, money you'll spend in the next five to fifteen years (typical example: saving for a child's college education), you want to have a mix of stocks and bonds that perhaps begins to shift more to bonds the closer you get to the anticipated spend date (e.g., college admission).

For the long-term bucket, money you don't anticipate needing for a long time (for example, for retirement), you want to invest it mostly in stocks (again, depending on your risk tolerance and your own likely behavior in a market downturn). Since this money is going to be used a long time in the future, you can ride out the ups-and-downs of the stock market and earn a higher rate of return by investing more in stocks and less in bonds. As you approach your spending date (e.g., retirement), you might start to shift your allocation to look more like your medium or short-term buckets.

It really is that simple. You don't have to be a fox and know lots of things about investing, just a hedgehog who understands their buckets and picks the right asset allocation. In the next section we'll talk more about how much of each bucket to put into stocks and how much into bonds, and what specific investments you should choose, but the takeaway from this section is pretty simple: **save as much as you can and invest it based on the time-horizon of when you are going to need to spend the money**.

> **Quick reminder**: The information in this book is not a substitute for researching and using your own critical thinking. Please contact a fiduciary to help clarify and confirm your plan before acting! We are not certified financial planners, but aim to help you start your education!

1.11: INVESTING: SPECIFIC INVESTMENTS

TL;DR: Decide on your asset allocation for each bucket, and invest in low-cost index funds. Keep it simple.

"Put 10% of the cash in short-term government bonds and 90% in a very low-cost S&P 500 index fund. (I suggest Vanguard's.) I believe the trust's long-term results from this policy will be superior to those attained by most investors —whether pension funds, institutions or individuals—who employ high-fee managers." — Warren Buffett

As discussed in the previous section, divide your investments into a short-term bucket (want to spend it in five years or less), a medium-term bucket (five to fifteen years), and a long-term bucket. For your short-term bucket, you want a more "conservative" asset allocation (bonds, certificates of deposit, and savings), for the medium-term bucket more of a balanced asset allocation (stocks and bonds), and for your long-term bucket a more "aggressive" allocation (more stocks). The specific allocation you decide on will depend on your risk tolerance, but the following is some general advice.

In general, humans are loss-averse, they worry more about losing (in this case, losing money) than winning, and will do whatever it takes to avoid that. As a result, most investors have an asset allocation that is too conservative. If you are a long-term investor (which you should be) and will not panic and sell before you need the money, then you should be invested mostly in stocks in your long-term bucket. In your short-term bucket, invest mostly in bonds (although as you get closer to the spend-date, consider certificates of deposit or your savings account for any new money).

For both stocks and bonds, you should invest in low-cost, diversified index funds. While no one controls what the market will return, we can control the fees we pay (which helps us earn what the market returns, which is typically enough for living our good life). While there are several good choices, it's best to keep it simple. For investments you have complete control over (typically your non-tax advantaged accounts, your Roth IRA, and your Traditional IRA if you have one), go with **Vanguard**. For your tax-advantaged accounts through your employer (401k/403b/457 and possibly an HSA), you will be limited by the choices the plan offers you. If Vanguard is a choice, go with them. If not, most plans have an **index fund choice from somebody**, so choose that (or the choice that's closest to that with the **lowest expense ratio**). While you can't control what the market does, you can control your expenses, which is why choosing low-cost index funds (which have lower expenses) will pay off in the long run.

> **Note**: There are good choices other than Vanguard, but Vanguard is consistently one of the best (or the best). It is the only mutual fund company owned by its customers (you), and this helps them keep fees low and always operate in your best interest.

So, what should your asset allocation look like? Again, it's going to vary, but here are some good baselines. For each of these, we take a "white-label" approach, by choosing the type of asset as opposed to a particular fund. This is helpful because within your employer-based plan you will likely have the choices of funds determined for you, so you can pick the fund(s) that most closely match the "white-label." For each "white-label" we also give the specific symbol for the Vanguard fund associated with it as a **reference** (you can use funds or ETFs, whichever is easier for you). We break down each bucket into different portfolio choices: a one fund, a target-date fund, a three fund, and a five fund choice. Most people will be best served with fewer funds, but if you just have to have a little more, the five fund choice is there for you.

Note: As you get closer to the time when you are needing to spend the money in the long-term bucket, you may want to start adjusting it closer to the short-term bucket asset allocation. That will really depend on your financial situation at that time and is beyond the scope of this book.

Short-Term Bucket

- **One Fund**: Total Bond Market Index Fund (VBTLX)

- **Target Date Fund**: Choose the closest date to when you want to spend the money (e.g., if you anticipate spending the money in 2026, choose a Target Date 2025 fund (VTTVX).

- **Three Fund**: Total Bond Market Index Fund (VBTLX), Certificates of Deposit (timed to redeem when you need to spend the money), Savings Account

- **Five Fund**: Total Bond Market Index Fund (VBTLX), Certificates of Deposit (timed to redeem when you need to spend the money), Savings Account, High-Yield Bond Fund (VWEAX), Total Stock Market Index Fund (VTSAX)

Medium-Term Bucket

- **One Fund**: Balanced Fund (VSMGX)

- **Target Date Fund**: Choose the closest date to when you want to spend the money (e.g., if you anticipate spending the money in 2026, choose a Target Date 2025 fund (VTTVX).

- **Three Fund**: Total Stock Market Index Fund (VTSAX), Total International Stock Index Fund (VTIAX), Total Bond Market Index Fund (VBTLX)

- **Five Fund**: Total Stock Market Index Fund (VTSAX), Total International Stock Index Fund (VTIAX), Real Estate Index Fund (VGSLX), Total Bond Market Index Fund (VBTLX), High-

Yield Bond Fund (VWEAX)

Long-Term Bucket

- **One Fund**: Total Stock Market Index Fund (VTSAX)

- **Target Date Fund**: Take the year you anticipate needing to spend the money (e.g., when you are going to retire), and add five or ten years. So, for example, if you anticipate retiring in 2050, perhaps pick a Target 2055 or 2060 account (TL;DR for the explanation of why you should add five or ten years).

- **Three Fund**: Total Stock Market Index Fund (VTSAX), Total International Stock Index Fund (VTIAX), Real Estate Index Fund (VGSLX)

- **Five Fund**: Total Stock Market Index Fund (VTSAX), Total International Stock Index Fund (VTIAX), Emerging Markets Stock Index Fund (VEMAX), Small Cap Value Index Fund (VSIAX), Real Estate Index Fund (VGSLX)

For all of the multiple fund choices, you would periodically **rebalance** between the different funds to stay within your risk tolerance (and to force you to "sell high, buy low" because you'd be selling the funds that went up the most and buying the ones that went up the least). Again, don't stress out about making these investment choices. If you focus on your savings rate, and start investing early, time is your ally. While it's unclear if he ever actually said it, Albert Einstein is purported to have said, "Compound interest is the most powerful force in the universe." Whether he said it or not, it is one of the most powerful forces in your financial universe. If you **save early**, **invest in index funds**, and **continue saving and investing throughout your life**, compound interest will take care of the rest.

1.12: INVESTING: WHAT TYPE OF ACCOUNTS TO INVEST IN

TL;DR: This can be really complicated, so tough to tl;dr it. In general, short and medium-term bucket investments will be in taxable accounts, and long-term bucket investments will be in tax-advantaged accounts.

"A tax loophole is something that benefits the other guy. If it benefits you, it's tax reform." — Senator Russell Long

This is a very difficult section to tl;dr, as your decisions will vary tremendously based on your goals, your current circumstances, and what options you have available to you based on your employment. Consider the following a general introduction and then see **fischlearning.com/tldr-wyoming** for resources to dive deeper.

Once you decide on your asset allocation and your various buckets, you then have to decide what types of accounts to invest in. Mainly, this is a decision about whether to invest in taxable accounts or tax-advantaged accounts (403b, Roth IRA, etc.), and then within those tax-advantaged accounts which type(s) to invest in.

In general, your short and medium-term bucket investments will be in taxable accounts (notable exception: college savings, more on that later). Your long-term bucket investments will be invested in a combination of taxable and tax-advantaged accounts, and most likely multiple types of tax-advantaged accounts. Your exact choices here will vary a lot depending on your individual circumstances and goals.

For example, if you want to retire early you will have a different mix of accounts than if you plan on retiring at a "regular" age. Or if your employer matches some of your contributions to your 401k/403b that might change your mix a bit. Similarly, if you get a pension from your employment, that can have dramatic effects on what you choose to do (and your asset allocation). But, in general, for **many** (but **not all**) folks, the priority order will be:

- 401k (403b/457) up to employer match

- HSA (if you are enrolled in a High-Deductible Health Care Plan)

- Traditional and/or Roth IRA

- Traditional and/or Roth 401k (403b/457) up to the maximum you're allowed (If you are a public employee with access to a 401k/403b **and** a 457, you can double the amount you invest as each has its own limit).

- Taxable brokerage account

Money that you invest in your Traditional 401k (403b/457) comes out pre-tax and then grows tax free and is then taxed when you withdraw it during retirement. By coming out pre-tax, it allows you to invest "more" because you are able to invest what you would've paid in federal and state (and maybe local) taxes. (Of course, Wyoming currently doesn't have state taxes.) And, if your employer matches any of your contributions, it's equivalent to getting a tax-free raise. In addition, because your contributions lower your adjusted gross income and taxable income, it can help qualify you for other tax breaks that you might not receive if you didn't invest in the 401k (e.g., Savers Credit, lower capital gains taxes, etc.).

Once you've invested at least enough to obtain your employer's match and if you have a High-Deductible Health Plan, then invest the next amount in your HSA. Recall that you can withdraw funds from your HSA to pay health expenses but, if you can manage to not use the money to pay current health care expenses, it's a great long-term investment vehicle because the money is never taxed (comes out pre-tax, grows tax-free, and withdrawal is tax free if used for health expenses down the road). If used this way, it's like a "stealth" retirement account - and the only one that is never taxed.

After you've invested in your HSA, then often the next thing to do is to max out your Traditional or Roth IRA. This is because if you choose some place like Vanguard and choose low-cost, diversified index funds, the fees you pay will likely be less than through your employer 401k/403b/457. Note that there are income limits for being able to contribute to a Traditional or Roth IRA, so you may not be able to take advantage of this.

After that, then make sure you have maxed out your 401k (403b/457) contribution (this is assuming the associated fees are not too high). If you are a public employee and have access to both a 401k/403b and a 457, realize that the maximum investment limits for those are separate, so you can invest in both (effectively doubling the amount you can invest pre-tax). Also, assuming the investment choices and fees are equal, public employees should usually fund a 457 before a 401k/403b, because it's easier to withdraw your money earlier if you need to.

Once you've maxed out your pre-tax accounts, then any remaining money you have to invest can be invested in a taxable brokerage account (again, in diversified, low-cost index funds at a vendor like Vanguard).

Again, a reminder that this is general advice and the priority order can be different depending on your individual circumstances, investment choices, and retirement age (see **fischlearning.com/ tldr-wyoming** for additional resources).

1.13: INVESTING FOR COLLEGE

TL;DR: For most people, investing in a 529 College Savings Plan, typically (but not always) in the state you live, is the best option for saving for college.

"An investment in knowledge always pays the best interest." — Benjamin Franklin

If you decide to have children you will likely want to start saving and investing some money to help pay for their possible college education. For most people a **529 plan** is the best way to save for a college education for your child(ren). Earnings in a 529 plan grow tax-free and withdrawals are not taxed as long as they are used for college expenses. Some states also offer some kind of state tax incentive on contributions.

You can invest in any 529 plan, not just the one offered by your state. If your state doesn't offer any special incentives, then shop around the other states and pick the plan that has the best choice of index funds with low expense ratios (**savingforcollege.com** is a great resource to help you learn more). (Wyoming no longer offers a state 529 plan, but you can still use most of the other states' plans. Nevada's plan is a good, low-cost choice.)

When it comes time to pay for college (tuition, books and fees, room and board), you can withdraw money from the 529 plan without any tax consequences. Keep in mind that you do want to optimize for any other tuition assistance that might be available for you. For example, right now you can get up to a $2,500 tax credit through the **American Opportunity Tax Credit** (phased out for higher incomes), but you can only get that credit if you don't use 529 money for $4,000 worth of expenses (the first $2,000 is dollar-for-dollar tax credit, the next $2,000 is $0.25 for each dollar of expenses tax credit). So, for many folks, paying $4,000 a year with regular savings (not from the 529 account) and then using 529 money for anything above that makes the most sense.

1.14: EMPLOYMENT

TL;DR: Spend the time to learn about the benefits your employer offers and then make the optimal choices. Many people don't think deeply enough about their choices or take full advantage of their benefits.

"Workin' 9 to 5, what a way to make a livin'
Barely gettin' by, it's all takin' and no givin'
They just use your mind and they never give you credit
It's enough to drive you crazy if you let it"
— Dolly Parton

There is lots of advice out there about what kind of job you should get. Some folks advocate pursuing your passion, others doing what you are good at, and still others to do whatever will make you the most money. No matter which approach you take, once you have a job then you want to maximize the financial benefit you receive from that job.

Obviously, pay is important. The higher your salary or hourly wage, the more control over your financial situation you'll have. In many jobs, you can do what's expected of you and be just fine. But in some jobs, if you go above and beyond, you can increase your pay. Often your best option is to invest in yourself, learning additional skills that will allow you to perform your job better or even advance to another job within (or outside of) the company. If you continue to grow, your pay will typically grow with you.

While pay is the obvious part of work that most people focus on, many folks only think about benefits when they first get a job (or when they complain about them). And, often, those benefit choices are made quickly and without a lot of thought because you're excited about the new job and just want to get started. It is really worth your time to set aside an hour or so and dive a bit deeper into your benefits.

As mentioned previously, choosing your insurance options should require a bit more thinking than simply choosing the lowest premium or the lowest out-of-pocket cost. Often a plan with higher deductibles (like a high-deductible health plan) is the unintuitively better choice. You also want to take advantage of any other benefits your employer offers, such as taking out your insurance premiums pre-tax, or taking advantage of flexible spending accounts (health care, limited purpose health care, dependent care spending, etc.), known collectively as Section 125 plans.

You definitely want to take advantage of any employer matching for a 401k/403b/457 or company stock purchase program. (And you want to review the previous investment sections when looking at the investment choices in your 401k/403b/457 plan.) Some employers even offer help with covering your commuting costs, such as discounts on public transportation.

Just a reminder to also think carefully about the location of your work compared to where you live. As mentioned previously, your daily commute has an outsized impact on both your happiness and your finances. The more you can minimize your commute, and perhaps eliminate the need to drive to work every day, the better off financially you will be.

We'd also highly recommend that if you have your own high school or college-aged children, have them **read Part 1 of this book**, and then discuss it with them. Or, alternatively, you could buy the standalone **TL;DR: Financial Literacy for Young (and Not-So-Young) Adults (bit.ly/fischtldr)**, which is essentially Part

1 of this book without the WRS references.

Many folks have to work in high school or college to help their family pay the bills. But, for students who are lucky and privileged enough to not have to use that money to pay the bills, they should seriously consider **opening and contributing to a Roth IRA** during these years. Because most students in high school or college will not make enough to owe any federal taxes, taking this opportunity to invest in a Roth IRA means that money will **never be taxed** (they might have to pay a small amount in state taxes depending on their state). And, because they're young, that leaves plenty of time for compound interest to do its magic. They should also consider talking with their parents about possibly matching some or all of their contribution to the Roth IRA (kind of like an "employer match," only from their parents), so that they still have some "spending" money. They should try to contribute as much as possible to their Roth IRA (up to the limit, which is currently their total earned income for the year up to $6,000 maximum, including any "match" from their parents).

Imagine the possibilities if they start their adult lives being financially literate. (See **bit.ly/teensandroth** for more on this.)

1.15: RETIREMENT

TL;DR: The key to a comfortable retirement is to save and invest early and let compound interest go to work.

"For it is in your power to retire into yourself whenever you choose."— Marcus Aurelius

We're only going to briefly mention retirement in this section, as we will delve more deeply into it in the following sections.

Having said that, the best way to assure that you will be able to retire comfortably when you want to is to start planning (and saving, and investing) **early**. If you follow the advice in this book, as well as learn a little bit more after this, you are well on your way. When you can retire depends on a variety of factors, but the most important one is how much you save (which, as discussed previously, is based on how much you spend). The more you save and invest - particularly if you start early and let compound interest do its magic - the earlier you will be able to retire. Note that you may not want to "retire early," but reaching a "**work optional**" stage of life earlier rather than later is appealing for most folks. (Again, it more likely allows you to live the life you want to live.) There is a whole community online known as the FIRE community (Financial Independence Retire Early) that you can explore if you want to learn more about reaching that work optional (financially independent) stage earlier.

PART 2: YOUR WRS BENEFITS

Note that this will not cover every intricacy and detail of your WRS benefits, but will cover the most important aspects. Please always check out **retirement.wyo.gov** or contact WRS directly with any questions (they are very, very helpful). Also keep in mind that WRS benefits can change over time.

2.1: WHAT IS WRS AND WHAT DOES IT PROVIDE FOR ME?

TL;DR: While most folks (correctly) focus on the defined benefit you will eventually get from WRS, you should also be aware of the survivor and disability benefits that are part of your membership.

The **Wyoming Retirement System (WRS)** was created in 1953 by the state of Wyoming to provide retirement benefits to all teachers and state employees in the state of Wyoming. It is designed as a **supplement** to your Social Security benefits and your personal savings. In general, Social Security is designed to replace about 40% of your pre-retirement income (at the "regular" retirement age of 67 for most folks), although this varies depending on your level of income. WRS can additionally replace much of your pre-retirement income depending on your years of service (the average annual benefit in 2020 was $22,128 with an average of 20.1 years of service). And then your personal savings and investments can help you bridge the gap between retiring from WRS-covered employment and the age at which you can start receiving Social Security.

WRS members work in all varieties of public service occupations, including teachers, police officers, firefighters, public health professionals, game wardens, accountants, professors, mechanics, and many others. WRS represents about 1 in

7 Wyoming residents. While the benefits are similar across membership categories, there are differences that can be important. For the rest of this book, we will focus solely on **Members in the Public Employee Pension Plan** (which covers about 86% of active WRS members).

WRS is a **Defined Benefit (DB) Plan**. A Defined Benefit Plan means that you receive a lifetime retirement benefit determined by a formula that is based on the number of **years of employment**, your **highest average salary (HAS)**, and the **age at which you retire**. This is in contrast to a **Defined Contribution Plan (DC)** like a 401k (or similar plan like a 403b/457), where your retirement benefit is dependent on how much you save and invest and how those investments grow. Defined Contribution Plans (DC) can be exhausted if money is withdrawn at an unsustainable rate.

Your lifetime benefit is paid for by contributions both you and your employer make to WRS, as well as the investment gains those contributions earn over time. There are over 80,000 members of WRS and it currently has about $9 billion in assets invested on behalf of its members. Because it invests on behalf of all those members, WRS has the advantage of being a truly long-term investor and can ride out the volatility that occurs in the market. Because WRS is so large, it is able to both invest at low cost and to invest in areas that are not available to you as an individual investor. Because they are a large, institutional investor, they are able to negotiate investment fees that are lower than what you can typically achieve on your own. They can also invest in areas such as real estate and private equity that are not available to you as an individual investor. All of these factors help WRS achieve higher returns (at the same or lower level of risk) than most individual investors. As an individual investor, you have to account for different risks that are very sensitive to your current age, the rest of your financial situation, and the state of the market. WRS, on the other hand, can invest on behalf of all of its members and its size allows for it to better weather the inevitable ups and downs of the markets.

Members of the Public Employee Pension Plan currently (as of July 1, 2021) contribute 9.25% of their salary (with 5.57% of your "contribution" paid by your employer), and your employer currently contributes 9.25% of your salary to WRS. These rates can change each year based on the funded status of the plan. The current funded status of the **Public Employee Pension Plan** is 73.2%, meaning that there is currently an unfunded liability which has to be paid off. Once that unfunded liability is (hopefully) paid off in the late 2040's, then both employee and employer contributions will likely drop, although that is not guaranteed. (Note that the total employee plus employer contribution is essentially all coming from the employer, so the distinction between the two is only important because the employee contribution counts as more of a liability for the plan because the employee can take that money with them if they leave.)

In addition to the Defined Benefit you receive upon retiring, WRS also offers **Disability** and **Survivor** benefits once you are vested, While most members (correctly) focus on the Defined Benefit piece of WRS, disability and survivor benefits are also really important and we will briefly take a look at them as well.

> **Quick reminder**: The information in this book is not a substitute for contacting the system. Please contact WRS to clarify and confirm your plan before acting!

2.2: WRS DEFINED BENEFIT PLAN

TL;DR: While most people know they get a pension from WRS, being more knowledgeable about how that pension is calculated can help you maximize your benefit amount and decide on the best time to retire.

While most WRS members know they have a "good" pension plan, they may not be aware of how good it is (and also how it might affect the rest of your financial planning decisions). The following will give the basics of how your benefit is determined and later we'll talk about some ways to optimize those benefits and some things to consider when deciding when to retire.

Tier 1 or Tier 2 Member

Determining whether you are a Tier 1 or Tier 2 member is **extremely important**, as your benefit amount and the age at which you are eligible to receive full benefits is different depending on which tier you are in. If you made a contribution to WRS **before September 1, 2012**, you are a **Tier 1** member. If you first contributed to WRS after **September 1, 2012**, then you are a **Tier 2 member**.

The benefit formula for everyone is:

Years of Service x Highest Average Salary (HAS) x Multiplier

Years of service are calculated similarly for each tier. For any month you work at least 86 hours, you are credited with one month of service (between 40-85 hours earns one-half month of service, and between 1-39 hours earns one-quarter month of service.)

But it's important to realize that the **HAS** and the **Multiplier** are different between Tier 1 and Tier 2, as well as when your full retirement age is. For these reasons, we will look at Tier 1 and Tier 2 separately.

Tier 1 Members

(contributed to WRS before September 1, 2012)

Multiplier

Tier 1 members earn a multiplier of **2.125% for their first 15 years** of service, then **2.25% for every year of service over 15 years**. So, for example, if you earn 20 years of service, your multiplier will be 43.125% (15 x 2.125% + 5 x 2.25%).

Highest Average Salary (HAS)

Your highest average salary is calculated by averaging your **highest 36 months** of contiguous acceptable salary. This is typically, but not always, your last 36 months. What is considered "acceptable" salary is defined in statute, but is generally any pay given for services rendered. Some examples of salary that is not included are reimbursement for unused sick or vacation leave, housing allowances, transportation expenses, early retirement incentives, bonuses, and generally anything that is considered a "fringe benefit."

There are also limits in place to prevent "spiking" of your salary during these 36 months to artificially increase your benefit.

Vesting

You are vested once you obtain at least **48 months of service credit**. You must be vested to earn a monthly benefit at retirement.

Retirement Eligibility Age

You are eligible for a **full retirement** if:

- You reach **age 60** and are **vested**

  or

- If your age plus your years of service add up to at least 85 (**Rule of 85**)

Your are eligible for a **reduced retirement** if:

- You reach **age 50** and are vested

  or

- You complete **25 years** of service at any age

If you take a **reduced retirement**, your benefit will be **reduced by 5% for each year you are below age 60.**

Tier 2 Members
(contributed to WRS after September 1, 2012)

Multiplier
Tier 2 members earn a multiplier of **2% for each year of service**. So, for example, if you earn 20 years of service, your multiplier will be 40% (20 x 2%).

Highest Average Salary (HAS)
Your highest average salary is calculated by averaging your **highest 60 months** of contiguous acceptable salary. This is typically, but not always, your last 60 months. What is considered

"acceptable" salary is defined in statute, but is generally any pay given for services rendered. Some examples of salary that is not included are reimbursement for unused sick or vacation leave, housing allowances, transportation expenses, early retirement incentives, bonuses, and generally anything that is considered a "fringe benefit."

There are also limits in place to prevent "spiking" of your salary during these 60 months to artificially increase your benefit.

Note: If you are vested (48 months of service), but have not reached 60 months of service, your HAS would be calculated with zeros for the months you are short of 60 months.

Vesting
You are vested once you obtain at least **48 months of service credit**. You must be vested to earn a monthly benefit at retirement.

Retirement Eligibility Age
You are eligible for a **full retirement** if:

- You reach **age 65** and are **vested**

   or

- If your age plus your years of service add up to at least 85 (**Rule of 85**)

Your are eligible for a **reduced retirement** if:

- You reach **age 55** and are **vested**

   or

- You complete **25 years of service** at any age

If you take a **reduced retirement**, your benefit will be **reduced by 5% for each year you are below age 65.**

Monthly Benefit Options

No matter whether you are Tier 1 or Tier 2, you have **eight different options** for how you take your retirement benefit that differ based on the **death benefit** that is provided when you die. You select the option at retirement and, once you've selected an option, you cannot change it. (There is also a ninth option, which is to take a lump-sum withdrawal, but we'll focus on the monthly benefit options.)

Option 1: Single Lifetime Benefit with Beneficiary

You get a monthly benefit amount based on the formula calculation, but if you die before the total of your paid out benefits exceeds your total contributions plus interest, your beneficiary receives the difference in a lump-sum payout. This balance is typically exhausted in the first 3-5 years of retirement. Your beneficiary does not receive any continuing monthly benefit.

Option 2: 100% Joint and Survivor Benefit

You get a monthly benefit amount lower than the formula calculation, but if you die before your beneficiary, that monthly benefit would continue until your beneficiary's death.

Option 2P: 100% Joint and Survivor Benefit with Pop-Up Provision

This is similar to Option 2, where your beneficiary would still receive your same monthly benefit if you die first. But your monthly benefit amount will be slightly smaller than Option 2, because if your beneficiary dies first, then your benefit will "pop-up" to the Option 1 amount.

Option 3: 50% Joint and Survivor Benefit

You get a monthly benefit amount lower than the formula calculation, but if you die before your beneficiary, your beneficiary will receive 50% of your monthly benefit until your beneficiary's death.

Option 3P: 50% Joint and Survivor Benefit with Pop-Up Provision
This is similar to Option 3, where your beneficiary would still receive 50% of your same monthly benefit if you die first. But your monthly benefit amount will be slightly smaller than Option 3, because if your beneficiary dies first, then your benefit will "pop-up" to the Option 1 amount.

Option 4A: 10-year Certain Benefit
You get a monthly benefit amount lower than the formula calculation that ends with your death. But if you die before you have received benefits for 10 years, your beneficiary will continue to receive benefits for the balance of the 10-year period.

Option 4B: 20-year Certain Benefit
You get a monthly benefit amount lower than the formula calculation that ends with your death. But if you die before you have received benefits for 20 years, your beneficiary will continue to receive benefits for the balance of the 20-year period.

Option 5: Single Lifetime Benefit without Beneficiary
This is the only benefit with a (slightly) higher amount than Option 1. You receive a monthly benefit for your lifetime, but there is no provision for any lump-sum benefit to your beneficiary if you die and haven't exhausted your contributions plus interest as in Option 1.

Self-Funded COLA Feature
WRS benefits **do not currently offer a cost-of-living-adjustment (COLA)**. The benefit you receive during your first month of retirement will **not** increase over time. There is a possibility that the state legislature will reinstate a COLA once the plan is fully funded, but that is unlikely to happen for many years.

You have the option to create your own COLA, by reducing your initial monthly benefit amount and then having it increase by a set amount (1%, 2% or 3%, depending on which option you choose) each year. This COLA kicks in on July 1st following the two-year anniversary of your retirement. (In other words, the COLA does not begin for at least two years after you've retired.) Then each July 1st after that, your benefit will increase by the percentage option you chose, and this will be compounded (so based on your previous year's benefit which might have already been increased by previous COLAs).

The trade-off here is that your monthly benefit will be lower for many years before the COLA increases help you "catch-up" to the regular benefit. But the advantage is that it allows you to better budget to help deal with the effects of inflation and, should you live longer than your life expectancy, you will eventually receive more benefits (and it acts as "longevity insurance").

Here's an **example** to give you an idea of how the various options might differ and how selecting a self-funded COLA might impact your monthly benefit. Please note this is **just an example** and your actual numbers will be different based on your formula calculation, any reduction due to a reduced retirement for retiring early, the age of your beneficiary, and the current actuarial assumptions for the WRS pension plan.

Tier 1, age 60, beneficiary age 60, $65,000 HAS, 30 years of service	Self-Funded COLA Percentage			
Option	Monthly Benefit (no COLA)	Monthly Benefit (1% COLA)	Monthly Benefit (2% COLA)	Monthly Benefit (3% COLA)
1	$3,554	$3,279	$3,009	$2,744
2	$3,222	$2,945	$2,674	$2,411
2P	$3,182	$2,900	$2,624	$2,356
3	$3,380	$3,103	$2,831	$2,567
3P	$3,361	$3,081	$2,805	$2,537
4A	$3,494	$3,225	$2,961	$2,702
4B	$3,343	$3,078	$2,820	$2,568
5	$3,561	$3,285	$3,014	$2,748

This example assumes an Option 1 benefit calculated at $3,554 per month, and shows what the other option benefits would be with no COLA, and then what each would be with a 1%, 2% or 3% self-funded COLA. Again, to be perfectly clear, this is just an example, and you must contact WRS to find out what your numbers would be. You can also go to **retirement.wyo.gov/en/ Members/Pension-Estimate** to do a rough pension estimate, or login to your WRS account to get one calculated on your actual numbers on file.

Taxes

Your WRS benefit is purchased with pre-tax money (with possibly a partial exception for years you purchase, more on that later), so therefore when you receive your benefit it is considered taxable income. This income is fully taxable but is not considered "earned income," therefore you can't shelter any of it by contributing to a 401k/403b/457/IRA/etc.

Because it's difficult to forecast the tax rates that will be in effect when you retire, and you may even move to a different state with different state tax rules (particularly relevant since Wyoming doesn't have a state income tax, but most states do), planning for this can be very tricky. Just keep in mind that if you anticipate a decent WRS benefit along with your Social Security benefit (which is mostly taxable), you will likely end up in a "medium" tax bracket, so that may affect other decisions you make like whether to contribute to a Traditional or a Roth IRA/401k/403b/457.

2.3: SURVIVOR AND DISABILITY BENEFITS

TL;DR: An underappreciated aspect of your WRS benefits is the survivor and disability benefits.

Survivor (death) benefits are just what they sound like, benefits that your survivors receive if you die **before retiring**. If you die before retirement, your survivors may be eligible for either a lump-sum payment or a monthly benefit. The rules around this are complicated, so contact WRS for the details, but we'll discuss this briefly.

Whether you are vested (48 months of service credit) or not at the time of your death makes a difference on what options your beneficiaries have.

Not Vested
Your beneficiary will receive a one-time lump-sum equal to **twice your account balance** at the time of your death. But, if you were hired **after** July 1, 2019, and you are **not actively employed** at the time of your death, your account balance will **not** be doubled.

Vested
Your beneficiary will receive a one-time lump-sum equal to **twice your account balance** at the time of your death. Your beneficiary **may** also be able to choose to receive a lifetime monthly benefit.

If they choose a lump-sum benefit, they have the option of choosing to roll over any pre-tax portion to a Traditional IRA or retirement plan (non-spouse beneficiaries can only roll it over to an IRA that follows inherited IRA rules.)

In order to receive a lifetime benefit, a spousal beneficiary must be of retirement age and must begin taking a benefit by the time the member (you) would have reached age 72.

For a non-spousal beneficiary to elect a lifetime benefit rather than a lump sum, the beneficiary must be at retirement age to begin the benefit within one year of the date of your death. Otherwise, the non-spousal beneficiary would only be eligible for the lump sum death benefit.

If you have designated multiple individuals as primary beneficiaries, monthly retirement benefits are not an option. In these cases, lump sum payments will be made to the beneficiaries in equal shares, unless otherwise specified in writing to WRS prior to your death. Monthly retirement benefits are also not an option if you have designated an entity, such as a trust or charity, as your beneficiary.

Disability benefits are what you get if you become disabled while working for a WRS employer. An important caveat is that you only qualify for disability benefits if you are a **contributing member** of WRS, have **10 or more years of service**, and **have not reached normal retirement age** (60 for Tier 1, 65 for Tier 2).

If you become incapacitated to the point you cannot perform your duties, you may be eligible for a disability retirement. A "total disability" means a condition rendering you unable to engage in any occupation for which you are reasonably suited by training or experience and which is expected to last at least 12 months. A "partial disability" means a condition rendering you unable to fulfill the occupation for which you are reasonably suited by training or experience, which is expected to last at least 12 months but still allows you to function in other employment.

Like Survivor Benefits, the rules around this are complicated, so contact WRS for the details. Note that both survivor and disability benefits are built into WRS, there is no "extra charge" for this benefit.

2.4: OPTIONAL LIFE INSURANCE

TL;DR: WRS also offers an optional life insurance benefit through the National Conference on Public Employee Retirement Systems.

WRS also offers an optional life insurance program through the National Conference on Public Employee Retirement Systems (**mybensite.com/wy**). For $16 a month, you get life insurance whose benefit decreases as you age (starting at $225,000 and eventually decreasing to $7,500). It also provides Accidental Death and Dismemberment Insurance and a small dependent life insurance.

Please keep in mind that you may be able to get better life insurance through your employer or on the open market, but this is a nice additional option that you have as part of your WRS membership.

2.5: PURCHASING SERVICE CREDIT

TL;DR: Many WRS members are unaware that they can purchase additional years in WRS, based on non-WRS covered employment, which can increase their defined benefit amount and perhaps allow them to retire earlier.

Many WRS members don't realize that they may be eligible to **purchase years of service credit**. This idea might be counterintuitive, but the idea is that if you've worked for a while in non-WRS-covered employment, this is an opportunity to "buy" those years into WRS. Once the years are bought, they act just like years you've worked for a WRS employer, which means that you will have more years that your defined benefit is based on and therefore your monthly benefit will be higher.

If you are a currently employed and vested member of the WRS Public Employee Pension Plan, you can make a one-time purchase of up to 5 years of qualified employment. Honorably discharged U.S. military veterans may make an additional one-time service purchase, with the total of both service purchases not to exceed eight years. Visit **retirement.wyo.gov/en/Members/Service-Purchase** to get a ballpark estimate of what credit would cost, but you must contact WRS to get an exact figure.

The cost to purchase service credit can vary widely depending on your salary, the type of credit, your years of service, and other details. When possible, most people choose to purchase service credit with pre-tax money, which means using money that you have already contributed to a Traditional 401k/403b/457 or IRA. You can also use post-tax money to purchase service credit. (The portion of your defined benefit that was purchased with post-tax money will not be taxed in retirement.)

Purchasing service credit is often not cheap, as the cost to purchase service credit is the actuarial cost of providing the future benefit resulting from the purchase and is calculated using your HAS, your age, and other factors. Having said that, this is often a great option for many educators to **turn a lump-sum into guaranteed income for life**.

The decision around purchasing is complicated and varies tremendously, but basically the tradeoff you are making is trading a chunk of money now (that you could possibly invest and make a lot of money with over time) for a guaranteed increased monthly income for life. For many people, that is a great tradeoff to make to know that you will have an increased monthly income. None of this is to say that purchasing years is right for everyone (life expectancy and joint life expectancy depending on the option you take is really important here), but for folks whose primary objective is to have more income/spending power (versus leaving a larger legacy), the behavioral economics of purchasing the years can be powerful. Also keep in mind the benefit of possibly retiring earlier (as it can negate the reduced retirement reduction).

WRS counselors are very helpful at not only helping you figure out how many years you can purchase and what the cost would be, but at helping you evaluate the pros and cons of purchasing. The great thing about WRS is that they are not trying to sell you anything, they get paid for giving good service, so their advice is not compromised by financial incentives to sell you something. We think everyone should at least explore purchasing service credit and get the details, even if you end up deciding not to purchase.

2.6: WORKING AFTER RETIREMENT

TL;DR: Once you retire and begin receiving a WRS benefit, you can return to work, but there are limitations if you return to a WRS-covered employer.

Once you are receiving a WRS retirement benefit, some members may choose to return to work. If you return to work with a **non-WRS-covered employer**, there are **no restrictions** on how much you can work and how much you can earn - your WRS benefit will be unaffected.

But if you return to work with a WRS-covered employer, it's a bit more complicated. There must be a **30-day break in service** between your retirement and returning to work. If you return to work and fill a vacant full-time position of a regular contributing employee, you are considered a "**rehired retiree**."

As a rehired retiree, you must choose whether to **continue to receive your benefit** and **not accrue additional service credit,** or to **stop receiving your benefit** and become an **active, contributing member again**. If you want to continue your benefit, **your employer must contribute both the employee and employer portion of the WRS contribution to WRS** (even though you are not receiving service credit). If you stop your benefit, then you accrue additional service credit and your retirement benefit will be **recalculated** upon your new retirement date (but you must keep the same benefit option and the same beneficiary you chose the first time).

While most people who retire from WRS probably don't wish to return to employment, it is a nice option should the financial need arise.

2.7: WRS SUMMARY

TL;DR: Knowledge (of your WRS benefits) is power.

These are the highlights of your WRS benefits, but in a book of this length we can't cover everything. So be sure to explore the WRS website or meet with a WRS counselor to get more or to clarify information. WRS is an unusual organization in many ways, one of the most prominent of which is how focused they are on customer service. They don't have to try to sell you anything, so their entire goal when working with you is to help you make better informed decisions. So don't hesitate to reach out to them via phone or an in-person (or virtual) visit, to ask anything from seemingly "simple" to very complex questions.

Many folks are unaware of all the benefits that WRS offers and the degree to which these benefits should influence the rest of your financial decisions. Part 3 will take a look at several of the financial areas from Part 1 and show you how your WRS benefits - in conjunction with your school district benefits - will likely change how you approach some of those decisions in order to optimize your finances.

PART 3: HOW TO OPTIMIZE YOUR FINANCIAL PLANNING TO TAKE ADVANTAGE OF YOUR WRS BENEFITS

This part focuses on how your WRS benefits - along with other benefits from your school district - impact many of the financial areas discussed in Part 1, and how you can optimize those decisions based on those benefits.

3.1: OPTIMIZING YOUR DEFINED BENEFIT

TL;DR: Now that you know more about how your defined benefit is calculated, here are some ways to optimize it.

There are two ways (at least) to optimize the defined benefit you will ultimately receive from WRS.

Purchase Service Credit
As discussed previously, for every year of service credit you purchase, you get an increased percentage of your HAS (or prorated for partial years). This may also allow you to retire earlier with either reduced or full retirement benefits. This not only gives you a bigger "paycheck" in retirement, but gives you much appreciated flexibility on when you can retire. Also keep in mind that depending on the death benefit option you choose, the impact might also apply to your beneficiary. (If you are a two-WRS family, then this can be fantastic in many, many ways.)

Maximize Your WRS-Includable Salary in Your HAS Years
The years that your HAS is calculated on are a great time to earn any extra money from your school district that might be available to you (life circumstances and energy level permitting). This can include anything from changing positions (from teacher to instructional coach or administrator for example), to taking on extra duties (coaching, department chair, mentoring), to working taking tickets or supervising athletic events or activities. You obviously have to evaluate if the money is worth your time, but keep in mind that not only are you earning those extra dollars for

those five years, but you will be getting a larger check for hopefully 30+ years in retirement.

Note: WRS does have provisions in place to prevent "spiking," so there are limits that apply to how much your salary can increase during your HAS years, so you may want to start earning more four (tier 1) or six (tier 2) or more years before your anticipated retirement.

3.2: OPTIMIZE YOUR VOLUNTARY RETIREMENT PLAN, HSA, AND 529 PLAN INVESTMENTS (ASSET ALLOCATION)

TL;DR: Because of your excellent defined benefit through WRS along with Social Security, you are able to invest more aggressively throughout your career (and even into retirement) and earn a higher long-term rate of return.

This is a tough one to discuss in a general way, as the "right" decisions will vary tremendously based on your individual circumstances. But everyone should likely be contributing to a 401k/403b/457 plan and possibly also an IRA outside of work. (And, if you have a High Deductible Health Plan, you should be trying to max out your HSA and invest that for the long term, too.) It's important to compare the offerings from any vendors your district has contracted with to offer 403b's or 457 plans with what you can invest in in your personal IRA. (See **Section 1.12** for the order in which you should fund these plans.)

Your Voluntary Retirement Plan (403b/457/IRA)

A 403b is the public employer equivalent of the 401k, it's an employer-sponsored savings plan for retirement. Public employers also have the option of offering a 457b plan (so you can tax-defer even more money if you are able), which is similar but offers some additional attractive options. The problem with 403b's (and some 457's), is that they often have fees that are way too high. Those fees often end up more than offsetting any tax advantages you get from using those accounts. (See **bit.ly/ tldr403b** for more.)

To help with this, WRS offers the **WRS 457 Deferred Compensation Program (retirement.wyo.gov/en/DC)**. All WRS members have access to this **optional** supplemental savings plan, in addition to whatever 403b and/or 457 plans your district may offer. Keep in mind that a 457 plan is a different "bucket" than a 403b plan, so you can contribute up to the maximum in **both** plans (currently $19,500 if you are under 50, $26,000 if you are over 50, so you can contribute up to $39,000 or $52,000, total, between the 403b and 457).

The WRS 457 plan is a good (not great) plan with reasonable fees. You will want to compare the fees in the WRS 457 plan with the fees in the plans offered by your district. The WRS 457 plan currently charges a 0.20% administrative fee (capped at $300 annually, which you would reach if you had $150,000 or more invested), and then you have to pay for the fees associated with the underlying investments. Right now those fund fees range between 0.01% and 0.56%, for total fees of 0.21% to 0.76%. You want to keep your overall fees as low as possible and, in general, want to keep them under 0.30% (preferably even lower).

When you are comparing your district's 403b/457 offerings to the offerings from the WRS 457 plan, you need to pay careful attention to the fees and investment choices your district vendor(s) offer. Because each district can (sometimes) negotiate different fees from a vendor, you can't always assume that the fees the vendor offers elsewhere are the same ones you have. Two excellent places to learn more about this are **403bwise.org** and **403bcompare.com**. In **general**, the following vendors are likely to be the only good district-level 403b/457 choices with relatively low fees and good investment choices:

- Aspire
- Fidelity Investments
- ICMA-RC
- TIAA
- T. Rowe Price
- Vanguard

For many folks (unless you get an employer match), the best option is to invest in an IRA (either Traditional or Roth, and preferably through Vanguard or someone similar). You can invest in low-cost, diversified index funds through Vanguard for less than 0.10% expense ratios, which is typically much less than you can through your 403b/457. Keep in mind, however, that there are income limits that might preclude you from investing in an IRA. They change each year, and there are different limits for Traditional vs. Roth, check the IRS website or just google to find the current year limits. Note that any pre-tax deductions to a traditional 401k/403b/457 reduces your income for this calculation, so often by contributing to a Traditional 401k/403b/457, you can lower your AGI enough to qualify to also contribute to an IRA. And, unfortunately, the total amount you can invest in an IRA each year is lower than what you can invest in a 401k/403b/457.

Once you've maxed out your personal IRA (assuming your income qualifies), then a 401k/403b/457 is another good option. Again, check with your district to see what they offer and compare it to the WRS 457 plan. And recall that you can contribute to **both** a 403b and a 457 plan at the same time. (Note: while 457 and 403b plans are very similar, if the fees are the same you generally want to pick a 457 plan, because it has more liberal withdrawal rules before the age of 59.5.)

There are also some tricky calculations to do around whether to contribute to Traditional plans or Roth plans. Contributing to Traditional plans gets you a tax break now and also lowers your adjusted gross income which can sometimes qualify you for IRA contributions and for other tax breaks that you might not get if you didn't contribute. But because you are going to get a very good defined benefit (if you work for your WRS employer(s) for a long enough time), and that defined benefit will be fully taxable income when you get it (and Social Security will be mostly taxable), realize that withdrawals that you ultimately make from a Traditional 401k/403b/457 plan will likely be taken at a higher marginal tax rate than you might be expecting. That sometimes can tip the scale in favor of doing a Roth contribution instead. (Since it's often hard to tell for sure, lots of people split their contributions between both to remain flexible based on tax policy in the future.)

Your Health Savings Account (HSA)

Many school districts in WRS offer access to a **High Deductible Health Insurance Plan**. As discussed in Part 1, many people are scared away from these plans because of the high deductible but, when you do the math, they are often cheaper than the non-high-deductible plans (and significantly cheaper during healthy years). This is due to a combination of you paying lower premiums and your district often contributing money to your HSA. If you can afford to max out your HSA each year and not spend from it (pay for any medical expenses out of pocket instead of from your HSA), you can also invest it and let it grow for the long term.

Your HSA in effect can turn into a "**stealth IRA**," only even better because this money is **never taxed**. Note that HSAs are "better" than either Traditional or Roth IRAs because they are **triple-tax advantaged**: contributions, earnings and withdrawals are never taxed as long as you use them for medical expenses (and you can "accumulate" medical expenses over time and reimburse yourself for them in the future). So, if you can afford to pay medical expenses just from your regular cash flow, don't tap into your HSA and just invest it for the long run like you would your 401k/403b/457, and then begin withdrawing it (for medical expenses) in retirement.

So, let's do a hypothetical to just give you an idea of what this could look like. Let's take a 25-year old teacher just starting to contribute to their HSA. Let's assume that in addition to the employer (district) contribution, they max out their HSA. Let's also assume they have a spouse and therefore are able to contribute $7,200 per year into their HSA. For simplicity's sake, we'll ignore that the $7,200 will go up over time and that they typically have to have a minimum amount kept in cash before they can invest (that will be more than made up for with the increases to the $7,200 limit in the future). We'll assume they invest monthly in the Vanguard Total Stock Market Index Fund (VTSAX), and we'll assume an 8% return per year. (Historically, the return would be higher than 8%, but going forward it may not be so going to be a bit conservative here.) We'll assume they continue to invest $7,200 a year for 40 years (until age 65, when they will be covered by Medicare), and then start withdrawing money for any accumulated or future health care expenses.

So, how much will they have? **$1.8 million**. Tax free (and the money has never been taxed). And it will continue to grow after that, since they are unlikely to pull the full $1.8 million right away. (And, at the historical return of closer to 10%, you'd have $3.2 million. Even at only 6%, you'd have over $1.1 million.)

Now, it may be unlikely that they'll continue to teach until age 65, so they may lose any employer contribution before age 65. But, even if they do, they can still contribute up to the maximum with their own money, so the numbers still work. And given the fact that the $7,200 maximum per year goes up over time, the final amount will likely be **well over $2 million**.

While not all teachers have the ability to max out HSA contributions, it is still smart to contribute anything you can. Even small investments compound and can grow large over time. If a retiree collects a monthly pension, has funds in a 403b/457/ IRA, and has consistently contributed to an HSA, this will provide a rock solid financial base that has lots of built in flexibility. (See **bit.ly/tldrhsa** for more.)

Your Asset Allocation and Risk Tolerance

One more consideration is *how* you invest your money in 401k/403b/457/IRAs/HSA/etc., whether they are Traditional or Roth. As discussed in Part 1, many people invest too conservatively for their retirement, not realizing that the long-term nature of their investments makes "aggressive" investments not as risky over the long-term. For WRS members (at least those who anticipate working a full career with an WRS-covered employer), this is even more true. Here's why.

Your WRS Defined Benefit is **guaranteed income for life**, along with Social Security which is also **guaranteed income for life** (with a small cost of living adjustment). As a result, in combination these function very much like the bond (fixed income) portion of your portfolio. Using the 4% rule of thumb (not really a "rule," but a good way to approximate), take your anticipated yearly defined benefit amount from WRS plus your anticipated Social Security benefit amount and multiply by 25. (If you have a spouse, do that for your **combined** amounts.)

For example, let's say you anticipate your yearly defined benefit from WRS to be $40,000 (not that unrealistic for a career teacher retiring in 2030, for example), and that you expect your Social Security benefit (at age 67) to be $26,000, for a combined total of $66,000. If you multiply that by 25, that's the rough "equivalent" of $1.65 million invested in bonds (4% of $1.65 million is $66,000 a year). To be clear, it's a "rough equivalent." On the negative side, when you die, at least some and likely a lot of the pension (depending on which option you choose) and some of Social Security (depending on a lot of factors) will stop, whereas if there's anything left in your bond portfolio that could be left to your heirs. But on the positive side, the pension and Social Security continues for your life expectancy, whereas if you spend down your bond portfolio to $0, not only will nothing be left for your heirs, but you'll be eating ramen noodles three times a day. (Another good way to think about a defined benefit plus Social Security is as **longevity insurance** - you can't outlive it, although eventually inflation will take its toll).

So if you're expecting a decent defined benefit and Social Security, and that translates into the equivalent of a huge investment in fixed income (bonds), then what should you be investing your money in? Your defined benefit plus Social Security (guaranteed income for life) means that your asset allocation - how you divide your investments between stocks (equities), bonds (fixed income) and perhaps other asset classes (real estate, cash, etc.) - can be **much more aggressive**. In **general**, that means that WRS members can invest more of their portfolio than most people can in "riskier" investments like stocks and less in "safer" investments like bonds. (Note that "riskier" and "safer" are historically a short-term distinction, over longer periods of time stocks have outperformed bonds so therefore might not be considered riskier in the long term.)

Now, to be perfectly clear, this depends on the rest of your financial situation and, crucially, on your **risk tolerance**. While over time stocks are very likely to outperform bonds, and while over time stocks have always gone up, stocks are also much more volatile than bonds and can also go down - and often by a lot (for example, by over 30% in March of 2020 and by about 50% in 2007-2009). So not only do you need to take into account the rest of your financial situation when making this decision, you have to take into account *your own likely behavior* should the stock market drop precipitously. If you suspect (or know) that you would panic and sell your stocks when the market drops that much, then you don't want your asset allocation to be so aggressive. By having more "safer" investments like bonds in your portfolio, you will be more likely (behaviorally) to "ride out" the drop in the market (with the trade off being lower total returns over time).

On the other hand, if you know that you can "ride out the lows," perhaps because you've done it before (2007-2009, or March 2020) or because you know that the mathematics has always worked out in the long run, then you should consider making your asset allocation much more "aggressive" (heavily weighted towards equities). Since your long-term bucket is going to be invested for a long enough period of time that you should be able to ride out the lows, and because you have a defined benefit that you can count on, you should even consider making your retirement investment portfolio 100% equities. That's not a typo, if you have a good defined benefit, you should **consider** making your long-term retirement investments 100% in stocks. (See **bit.ly/tldrtarget** for more.)

Because you will not be completely relying on these investments to live on (because of your defined benefit plus Social Security), you won't find yourself in the situation of "spending down" your investments too quickly if you happen to retire during a bear (down) market. You can simply cut down on some of your "extra," discretionary spending until the market recovers. For example, perhaps you travel less if the market happens to be way down just after you retire, and then start travelling more once it recovers. On the other hand, if the market is not down a lot right after you retire, you are likely to have a lot more available to spend because you've invested more aggressively (and then you can just cut back some in the future should the markets drop a lot later).

We want to be perfectly clear here, this is a decision you need to **think about carefully**. There is no "one size fits all" advice that is going to apply to everyone. But many folks want to be told some specifics, so we'll do our best. So, if you have a good defined benefit (and especially if you are a two-WRS family with two good defined benefits) here is one way to perhaps help you decide where you fall based on your risk tolerance.

High Risk Tolerance: *"Even if my retirement portfolio were to drop by 50% like it would have in 2007-2009, I would still ride it out and not sell my stocks at the bottom of the market."*

If you truly think the above is true, either because you had a significant portfolio in 2007-2009 and you didn't sell or because you are very, very confident you would not if (when) this happens again, then you have a high risk tolerance and you should *consider* investing in 100% equities in your retirement portion of your portfolio. Here's what that might look like in the WRS 457 Plan, in your Traditional or Roth IRA at Vanguard, and in a 403b/457 offered by a vendor through your district (these are just examples, with expense ratios noted).

Note: All WRS 457 expense ratios below include the 0.20% administrative fee, but that fee is capped at $300 annually, which you would reach at $150,000 in investments. So if you have more than $150,000 in the WRS 457 plan, your expense ratios would be slightly lower than the ones indicated.

WRS 457 (expense ratios below include the 0.20% admin fee)
75% WRS Large Cap U.S. Equity Fund (0.21%)
25% WRS LifePath Index 2065, or latest date available if you are reading this further into the future (0.28%)

Vanguard Traditional and/or Roth IRA
40% Vanguard Total Stock Market Index Fund (VTSAX, 0.04%)
30% Vanguard Small Cap Value Index Fund (VSIAX, 0.07%)
30% Vanguard Total International Stock Index Fund (VTIAX, 0.11%)

Other 403b/457/HSA Vendor

This depends on what the vendor offers, but look for index funds with low expense ratios
40% Total Stock Market Index Fund or S&P 500 Index Fund (varies)
30% Small Cap or Small Cap Value Index Fund (varies)
30% Total International Stock Index Fund (varies)

Rebalancing
Because the three different funds will grow at different rates, you would want to periodically **rebalance** between the three funds to get you back to your original percentages of asset allocation between the funds. This keeps you within your asset allocation and forces you to "sell high(er), buy low(er)." There are two ways to consider doing this.

Easier: Once a year check your portfolio and rebalance back to the original percentages.

Harder (but not hard): Set up percentage bands. For example, a good rule of thumb might be to rebalance any time one of your funds is more than 4% different than your allocation. For example, if your Vanguard Total Stock Market Index Fund grew to more than 44% (or less than 36%) of your total portfolio, then you would rebalance. (Same idea for the other two funds.) While this takes a bit more effort than rebalancing once a year, some research has indicated that you could earn a bit more over time because it can let your "winners run" a bit longer before rebalancing.

Medium Risk Tolerance: *"Even if my retirement portfolio were to drop by 33% like it would have in March of 2020 due to the Covid pandemic, I would still ride it out and not sell my stocks at the bottom of the market."*

If you truly think the above is true, either because you had a significant portfolio in March 2020 and you didn't sell or because you are very, very confident you would not if (when) this happens again, then you have a medium risk tolerance and you should consider investing your retirement portion of your portfolio in such a way that equities are overweighted (but not 100%). Here's what that might look like in the WRS 457 Plan, in your Traditional or Roth IRA at Vanguard, and in a 403b/457 offered by a vendor through your district (these are just examples, with expense ratios noted).

WRS 457 (expense ratios below include the 0.20% admin fee)
50% WRS Large Cap U.S. Equity Fund (0.21%)
50% WRS LifePath Index. Pick the fund that is roughly 10 years past the year you anticipate retiring. So if you are anticipating retiring in 2040, pick the 2050 fund. (0.28%)

Vanguard Traditional and/or Roth IRA
50% Vanguard Total Stock Market Index Fund (VTSAX, 0.04%)
50% Vanguard Target Retirement Date Fund. Pick the fund that is roughly 10 years past the year you anticipate retiring. So if you are anticipating retiring in 2040, pick the 2050 fund. (0.15%)

Other 403b/457/HSA Vendor
This depends on what the vendor offers, but look for index funds with low expense ratios
50% Total Stock Market Index Fund or S&P 500 Index Fund (varies)
50% Target Retirement Date Fund. Pick the fund that is roughly 10 years past the year you anticipate retiring. So if you are anticipating retiring in 2040, pick the 2050 fund (varies)

Rebalancing
Just as with the High Risk Tolerance, you would want to periodically rebalance using one of the two methods described previously.

Lower Risk Tolerance: *"Even if my retirement portfolio were to drop by 15% like it would have at some point during most years the stock market has been around, I would still ride it out and not sell my stocks at the bottom of the market."*

If you truly think the above is accurate, either because you've had a significant portfolio for a while and you didn't sell when the market periodically corrects, or because you are very, very confident you would not when this happens again (it happens fairly often), then you have a lower risk tolerance and you should consider investing your retirement portion of your portfolio in such a way that equities are overweighted (but not as overweighted as the Medium Risk Tolerance). Here's what that might look like in the WRS 457 Plan, in your Traditional or Roth IRA at Vanguard, and in a 403b/457 offered by a vendor through your district (these are just examples, with expense ratios noted).

WRS 457 (expense ratios below include the 0.20% admin fee)
25% WRS Large Cap U.S. Equity Fund (0.21%)
75% WRS LifePath Index. Pick the fund that is roughly 10 years past the year you anticipate retiring. So if you are anticipating retiring in 2040, pick the 2050 fund. (0.28%)

Vanguard Traditional and/or Roth IRA
25% Vanguard Total Stock Market Index Fund (VTSAX, 0.04%)
75% Vanguard Target Retirement Date Fund. Pick the fund that is roughly 10 years past the year you anticipate retiring. So if you are anticipating retiring in 2040, pick the 2050 fund. (0.15%)

Other 403b/457/HSA Vendor
This depends on what the vendor offers, but look for index funds with low expense ratios
25% Total Stock Market Index Fund or S&P 500 Index Fund

(varies)

75% Target Retirement Date Fund. Pick the fund that is roughly 10 years past the year you anticipate retiring. So if you are anticipating retiring in 2040, pick the 2050 fund. (varies)

Rebalancing
You would want to periodically rebalance using one of the two methods described previously.

Very Low Risk Tolerance: *"I know that I will likely panic and sell if I check my retirement portfolio occasionally and it has dropped significantly."*

If this applies to you, then you should just pick a Target Date fund and then forget about it. It will rebalance for you and, because you don't have to check your balance, it should be easier to avoid panicking. Here's what that might look like in the WRS 457 Plan, in your Traditional or Roth IRA at Vanguard, and in a 403b/457 offered by a vendor through your district (these are just examples, with expense ratios noted).

WRS 457 (expense ratios below include the 0.20% admin fee) 100% WRS LifePath Index. Pick the fund that is roughly 10 years past the year you anticipate retiring. So if you are anticipating retiring in 2040, pick the 2050 fund. (0.28%)

Vanguard Traditional and/or Roth IRA
100% Vanguard Target Retirement Date Fund. Pick the fund that is roughly 10 years past the year you anticipate retiring. So if you are anticipating retiring in 2040, pick the 2050 fund. (0.15%)

Other 403b/457/HSA Vendor
This depends on what the vendor offers, but look for index funds with low expense ratios

100% Target Retirement Date Fund. Pick the fund that is

roughly 10 years past the year you anticipate retiring. So if you are anticipating retiring in 2040, pick the 2050 fund. (varies)

Rebalancing

You would **not** need to rebalance because the fund does it for you and you just have the one fund.

"Never" Sell

No matter which risk tolerance you fall under, your strategy (in your long-term bucket) should be to **never sell** (except when you are rebalancing between your existing funds). Once you've picked your strategy, **stick with it until you are retired** and start withdrawing the money. (At that point, you might consider shifting your asset allocation a bit, but that's beyond the scope of this book.) There is nothing more destructive to a retirement portfolio than panic selling when the market is at its bottom. Make sure you are invested in a way that is consistent with your risk tolerance.

PART 4: SCENARIO PLANNING

Part 4 looks at several different "life scenarios" for WRS members as examples of how you might combine Parts 1 through 3 into a coherent retirement plan.

4.1: PLAUSIBLE PATHS

TL;DR: Some important considerations as you chart your possible path to and through retirement.

The following are some example retirement scenarios for WRS members. While they are not random (we did put some thought into what might be some likely scenarios), they are simply a few examples to illustrate the concept. Please don't feel constrained by them or that one of them must be the "right" scenario for you. Think of them as brainstorming; looking at the possibilities in order to start thinking about what's right for you.

It's also important to realize that, like all scenarios, these will change based on the assumptions that have been made (and, by necessity, there are lots and lots of assumptions involved and at least some of them will likely be different by the time you retire). It's best to think of these as **"plausible paths,"** a reasonable outline of paths you might take in order to live the life you want and retire at the age you desire. They aren't meant to be prescriptive, but rather guides to help you make choices and decisions along the way. And, rest assured, you can completely ignore these scenarios and simply learn from - and act upon - the advice in the rest of this book independently of these scenarios.

A Note About Social Security: While you may be able to retire and get a benefit from WRS earlier than age 62, Social Security is a different story. The earliest you can receive your Social Security benefits is at age 62, and that is at a very reduced amount (think of it as similar to a WRS "reduced retirement"). For most folks reading this book (anyone born 1960 or later), the full retirement age for Social Security is age 67 (when you get your "regular" benefit). And, if you can wait to draw your Social Security until age 70, you get a higher benefit. The longer you can wait to draw Social Security (up until age 70), the higher your benefit will be.

This means there are many WRS members who will retire before they will start drawing their Social Security, which means there will be a "gap" where they will have to live off their WRS benefits (and any savings and investments they have, plus perhaps a spouse's income or retirement income) until they age into their Social Security benefit. This is not necessarily a problem, but it is something that you have to plan for if this applies to you.

Keep in mind that while you have the option of starting Social Security as early as age 62 it's ideal, if possible, to wait until age 67 or 70. If you start drawing Social Security before age 67, it will be at a reduced benefit compared to your full retirement age of 67 (and even more compared to starting at age 70).

Another great resource to try out different scenarios is **opensocialsecurity.com.**

4.2: THE SCENARIOS

TL;DR: By looking at some different career length and retirement scenarios, you can make decisions along the way that can help you achieve your goals and live your good life.

Each of the following scenarios will look at an educator ending their WRS-covered job at a specific combination of **age, years of service, highest average salary**, and the **percent of highest average salary** they are trying to replace (live on) in retirement. None of the scenarios assume you work (part-time or full-time) after retiring from education, but keep in mind that is always an option to supplement your income/spending, or just because you want to.

Please note:

- The age you stop working at your WRS-covered job and the age you start receiving pension benefits from WRS **may not be the same** depending on what age you want to retire.

- We assume your investments earn a **7% annual return** over time (invested in tax-advantaged, low-cost, diversified, equity index funds).

- For our **base case (initial numbers in each spreadsheet)**, we will also project forward from the start of the educator's career in terms of their investment in tax-advantaged accounts. In other words, we will start with an initial balance of $0 in their tax-advantaged account, and assume they will invest the same amount each month for the rest of their working career. Since most folks reading this will not be in this position, you can change those numbers in each spreadsheet to match your current situation (the current balance in your tax-advantaged account, as well as your current - or projected - monthly investments going forward for the remaining years until you retire from WRS-covered job.)

• The amount of replacement income one needs (percent of final average salary) **varies tremendously** based on **age, individual circumstances**, your **values and lifestyle preferences**, and **many other factors**. A conventional "rule of thumb" is that you need 80% of your final salary in retirement, but we feel this paints with an overly broad brush. Some folks need 100% (or even more) of their final average salary, others only need 50% (or even less). For each scenario we try to pick a "plausible" percentage, but you can (and should) adjust as necessary. You can modify the spreadsheets to change the assumptions (green cells) to fit what you feel is reasonable for you and see how they work out.

• Our base case assumes a **2% increase** (for inflation) in the amount of money you need to live on each year **through age 65**, then a **1% increase each year after that** (lower due to health insurance costs and discretionary expenses likely declining).

• An important note about **"sequence of return risk" (investopedia.com/terms/s/sequence-risk.asp)**. "Sequence of return risk" is the risk retirees face if they have several years of bad returns (losses) when they first retire, so that their first few years of withdrawals when combined with the losses from the market combine to dramatically decrease the balance in their retirement savings. Because of the sometimes dramatic drawdown that can occur in this situation, their retirement accounts are unable to recover from the initial poor returns even with subsequent good returns, because they have to continue withdrawing from the lower overall balance, so there is less room for compound interest to do its work.

For example, if the market were to drop by 30% in your first year of retirement, drop 5% the following year, and then drop 1% the third year, you only have about 66% of your original balance. But if you also withdrew 5% each year for living expenses, you would be at about 56% of your original balance, and the same dollar amount that you withdrew the first year at 5% of your balance is now a 9% withdrawal of this new, lower balance. That level of withdrawal is typically not sustainable.

For folks with a good pension, this risk is at least somewhat (and sometimes completely) mitigated because you have most (or all) of what you need to live on coming in from your pension (which is guaranteed and your benefit is not subject to "drawdown," and therefore not subject to sequence risk), and you are not depending on your investments to pay the day-to-day bills. Should you have a few down years in the market, you can just choose not to make any extra withdrawals from your investments and just spend your pension check. If you have good investment years, or if your investments recover after a few bad years, then you can pull from your investments for more discretionary spending.

But it's important to recognize the sequence risks involved. In some of our scenarios we are relying more on withdrawals from investment accounts, either before the individual can start drawing their Social Security and/or to supplement the pension. The three best ways to address sequence risk are to work longer and get a larger pension, save and invest more in your tax-advantaged account(s) so that you have more to draw from, or to be able to be flexible in your spending and spend less if the markets do poorly for a few years. How comfortable you are with the sequence of return risk for your particular situation will determine whether you feel the need for one or more of those options.

- Educators typically have access to a **403b** tax-advantaged account through their district and definitely have access to a **457 through WRS** as well. **All things being equal (fees, investment choices)**, educators should **fund the 457 first** (and then invest additional money in the 403b after maxing out the 457). The reason is that you are allowed to access money in a 457 before age 59.5 **without penalty** if you leave your employer, whereas in the 403b you have to wait until age 59.5. (There is the "rule of 55" for a 403b that says if you retire at age 55 or later you can access it without penalty before age 59.5, but that doesn't apply if you retire before age 55.) Because some educators will retire before age 59.5 (and possibly even before age 55), having the extra flexibility of tapping into the 457 prior to 59.5 is welcome. For all of our scenarios, we assume the educator is at least 55 when they retire, so they could withdraw from either a 403b or 457. If there is a chance you will retire before age 55, then you would need to use a 457 or a taxable brokerage account if you wanted to access funds before age 59.5 without penalty.

- Our base case is assuming you take the **Option 1 Benefit**. If you take a **different option** (which many of you will), you will need to adjust your pension amount downward.

- Our base case assumes a highest average salary of $70,000 since many Wyoming salary scales seem to top out around 20 years of service and around $70,000. This obviously might be different for you, so be sure to adjust the spreadsheets as necessary.

- These scenarios are in **today's dollars** and are based on today's salary schedules. Keep in mind that over time the salary schedules themselves will increase, but so will the cost of living. Since we can't predict which will increase more, it's best to just think about it in today's dollars.

As with all assumptions, ours could be wrong in small or large ways, and are simplified, and these are not the only choices you could make to end up with these results. But we feel they are reasonable assumptions (**"plausible paths"**) to give you some direction and some food for thought about possibilities for your own path.

Each scenario has an accompanying spreadsheet, which you can access at **fischlearning.com/tldr-wyoming**. Each spreadsheet is already filled in with our base assumptions. Any green cells are cells that you can change and the rest of the spreadsheet will adjust (you'll have to make a copy of the spreadsheet first before you can edit it). Don't change any of the white cells as they have formulas in them (unless you understand the formulas and are comfortable changing them). If you totally mess up a spreadsheet, don't worry, you can always go to the revision history and go back to the original, or return to our original and make another copy.

Scenario 1: Tier 1, Retire at Age 55, 30 Years of Service, Meets Rule of 85

Our first scenario looks at a career Tier 1 educator who wants to stop working at an WRS-covered job at the fairly early **age of 55 and who meets the Rule of 85 (so they get a full pension)**. As you might expect, someone wishing to retire at age 55 has to do things a bit differently than others, including **consistently saving and investing a decent amount in their tax-advantaged accounts** throughout their career, and controlling their spending in retirement. Crucially, this likely includes starting investing when they first begin teaching, although it is very possible to start later and end up in the same place, as long as you save and invest more (sometimes significantly more) later in your career.

Since you cannot start drawing Social Security until age 62 (and preferably not until age 67 or 70), this scenario relies on the educator filling the "gap" years between stopping working and drawing Social Security by drawing down their tax-advantaged investment account(s). Once they start receiving Social Security, then the remaining balance in the investment account is tapped to help supplement their pension.

Here are the assumptions we've made for the base case for this scenario:

1. **Stop Working at an WRS-covered job**: Age 55
2. **Start Drawing Pension**: Age 55
3. **Years of Service**: 30
4. **Multiplier**: 65.625%
5. **Current Balance in tax-advantaged investment account (403b/457/IRA)**: $0
6. **Monthly Investment in tax-advantaged investment account (403b/457/IRA)**: $350 ($4,200/year)
7. **Years Remaining to Invest**: 30
8. **Annual Return on investments**: 7%
9. **Highest Average Salary**: $70,000
10. **Replacement Income**: 85% of Highest Average Salary
11. **Yearly Increase in Retirement Income**: 2% through age 65, 1% after age 65
12. **Social Security Replacement Percentage**: 37%
13. **Age Begin Drawing Social Security**: 67
14. **Annual Reduction in Benefit**: 0%

Visit **fischlearning.com/tldr-wyoming** and click on the link for Scenario 1 to see the spreadsheet that illustrates this scenario with the above assumptions. Remember, you can change any of the numbers in the **green shaded cells** if you want to change any of the assumptions.

As you can see from the spreadsheet, this allows the educator to live on **$59,500 the first year after they stop working in an WRS covered job**, which is **85% of their highest average salary**. (Again, you can change any of those assumptions, including the final average salary and the percent of that you need to live on.) We assume that someone who wants to retire this early is comfortable living on a bit less and/or has adequately saved and invested in order to prepare for this moment. We've initially populated the spreadsheet with a starting balance of $0 in their investment account and then have them contribute $350 per month for the rest of their career. Since most of you are likely part way through your career, you can change those to whatever your current balance is, the number of years you have left in your career, and how much you are investing - or project you will invest - each month to match your situation.

They do not start drawing Social Security until age 67, so they need to withdraw from their investment account to make up the difference between their pension and what they need to live on. These withdrawals start at about 3.4% of their balance and increase to about 5.3% of their balance at age 66. Withdrawals that high may not be sustainable over time, but they don't have to be, because once they start receiving Social Security at age 67, they will need to withdraw very little from their investment accounts.

You'll also see that, based on the return assumption, the balance in their tax-advantaged account (403b/457/IRA) gets really large over time. But, again, note the information about **sequence of return risk** mentioned previously. If those larger drawdowns in those first years before Social Security kicks in are combined with poor market returns, the balance in the 403b could be dramatically lower (and even go to zero). Should you choose a scenario such as this one, you'll have to determine your comfort level with this scenario as we've laid it out and make adjustments as necessary (work longer, save/invest more, and/or spend less).

On the other hand, if you have a positive sequence of returns at the beginning of your retirement under this scenario, then your balance would increase as shown (or perhaps even more quickly), and you could then choose to withdraw - and spend - more than indicated in the spreadsheet. (Or, alternatively, you could start with a lower balance in your tax-advantaged account, but that does increase your exposure to sequence of return risk.) We think planning on a base spending level that you can live on makes sense and then, if the market does well, you can choose to increase your discretionary spending.

The bottom line for this scenario is that it is very possible for an educator to retire at age 55 if they meet the Rule of 85 and make choices along the way that grows their investments. They need to start investing as much as they can as early as they can, and increase that investment when they are able to, and make realistic projections about how much they will have accumulated in their tax advantaged accounts by age 55. They also need to make realistic assumptions about how much they will need to live on in retirement, by avoiding lifestyle creep and being able to live on a bit less than they were earning at the end of their career (or have a much larger balance in their 403b account when they retire so that they can withdraw more to support their spending).

Scenario 2: Tier 1, Retire at Age 55, 23 Years of Service, Does Not Meet Rule of 85

Our second scenario looks at a Tier 1 educator who wants to stop working at a WRS-covered job at the fairly early **age of 55 and who does not meet the Rule of 85 (so they get a reduced pension)**. As you might expect, someone wishing to retire at age 55 with a reduced pension has to do things a bit differently than others, including **consistently saving and investing a large** amount in their **tax-advantaged accounts throughout their career**, and **controlling their spending in retirement**. Crucially, this likely includes starting investing when they first begin teaching, although it is very possible to start later and end up in the same place, as long as you save and invest more (sometimes significantly more) later in your career.

Since you **cannot start drawing Social Security until age 62 (and preferably not until age 67 or 70),** this scenario relies on the educator filling the "gap" years between stopping working and drawing Social Security by drawing down their tax-advantaged investment account(s). Once they start receiving Social Security, then the remaining balance in the investment account is tapped to help supplement their pension.

Here are the **assumptions** we've made for the base case for this scenario:

1. **Stop Working at a WRS-covered job**: Age 55
2. **Start Drawing Pension**: Age 55
3. **Years of Service**: 23
4. **Multiplier**: 49.875%
5. **Current Balance in tax-advantaged investment account (403b/457/IRA)**: $0
6. **Monthly Investment in tax-advantaged investment account (403b/457/IRA)**: $1,000 ($12,000/year)
7. **Years Remaining to Invest**: 23
8. **Annual Return on investments**: 7%
9. **Highest Average Salary**: $70,000
10. **Replacement Income**: 80% of Highest Average Salary
11. **Yearly Increase in Retirement Income**: 2% through age 65, 1% after age 65
12. **Social Security Replacement Percentage**: 37%
13. **Age Begin Drawing Social Security**: 67
14. **Annual Reduction in Benefit**: 25%

Visit **fischlearning.com/tldr-wyoming** and click on the link for

Scenario 2 to see the spreadsheet that illustrates this scenario with the above assumptions. Remember, you can change any of the numbers in the **green shaded cells** if you want to change any of the assumptions.

As you can see from the spreadsheet, this allows the educator to live on **$56,000 the first year after they stop working in a WRS covered job**, which is **80% of their highest average salary**. (Again, you can change any of those assumptions, including the final average salary and the percent of that you need to live on.) We assume that someone who wants to retire this early is comfortable living on a bit less **and** has adequately saved and invested in order to prepare for this moment. We've initially populated the spreadsheet with a starting balance of $0 in their investment account and then have them contribute $1,000 per month for the rest of their career. Since most of you are likely part way through your career, you can change those to whatever your current balance is, the number of years you have left in your career, and how much you are investing - or project you will invest - each month to match your situation.

They do not start drawing Social Security until age 67, so they need to withdraw from their investment account to make up the difference between their pension and what they need to live on. These withdrawals start at a bit more than 4.6% of their balance and increase to about 5.6% of their balance at age 66. Those levels of withdrawals are not sustainable over a long period of time, but they don't have to be, because once they start receiving Social Security at age 67, they will need to withdraw much less from their investment accounts.

You'll also see that, based on the return assumption, the balance in their tax-advantaged investment account (403b/457/IRA) gets really large over time. But, again, note the information about **sequence of return risk** mentioned previously. If those larger drawdowns in those first years before Social Security kicks in are combined with poor market returns, the balance in the 403b could be dramatically lower (and even go to zero). Should you choose a scenario such as this one, you'll have to determine your comfort level with this scenario as we've laid it out and make adjustments as necessary (work longer, save/invest more, and/or spend less).

On the other hand, if you have a positive sequence of returns at the beginning of your retirement under this scenario, then your balance would increase as shown (or perhaps even more quickly), and you could then choose to withdraw - and spend - more than indicated in the spreadsheet. (Or, alternatively, you could start with a lower balance in your tax-advantaged account, but that does increase your exposure to sequence of return risk.) We think planning on a base spending level that you can live on makes sense and then, if the market does well, you can choose to increase your discretionary spending.

The bottom line for this scenario is that it is very possible for an educator to retire at age 55 even if they don't meet the Rule of 85, as long as they make choices along the way that grows their investments. They need to **start investing as much as they can as early as they can**, and **increase that investment when they are able to**, and make realistic projections about how much they will have accumulated in their tax advantaged accounts by age 55. They also need to **make realistic assumptions about how much they will need to live on in retirement,** by avoiding lifestyle creep and being able to live on a bit less than they were earning at the end of their career (or have a much larger balance in their 403b account when they retire so that they can withdraw more to support their spending).

Scenario 3: Tier 1, Retire at Age 60, 20 Years of Service

Our third scenario looks at a Tier 1 educator who wants to stop working at a WRS-covered job at **age 60 and has 20 years of service (so they get a full pension)**.

While you can **start drawing Social Security at age 62, it's advantageous to wait until age 67 (or 70),** so this scenario relies on the educator filling the "gap" years between stopping working and drawing Social Security at age 67 by drawing down their tax-advantaged investment account(s). Once they start receiving Social Security, then the remaining balance in the investment account is tapped to help supplement their pension.

Here are the **assumptions** we've made for the base case for this scenario:

1. **Stop Working at a WRS-covered job**: Age 60
2. **Start Drawing Pension**: Age 60
3. **Years of Service**: 20
4. **Multiplier**: 43.125%
5. **Current Balance in tax-advantaged investment account (403b/457/IRA)**: $0
6. **Monthly Investment in tax-advantaged investment account (403b/457/IRA)**: $1,200 ($14,400/year)
7. **Years Remaining to Invest**: 20
8. **Annual Return on investments**: 7%
9. **Highest Average Salary**: $70,000
10. **Replacement Income**: 90% of Highest Average Salary
11. **Yearly Increase in Retirement Income**: 2% through age 65, 1% after age 65
12. **Social Security Replacement Percentage**: 37%
13. **Age Begin Drawing Social Security**: 67
14. **Annual Reduction in Benefit**: 0%

Visit **fischlearning.com/tldr-wyoming** and click on the link for Scenario 3 to see the spreadsheet that illustrates this scenario with the above assumptions. Remember, you can change any of the numbers in the **green shaded cells** if you want to change any of the assumptions.

As you can see from the spreadsheet, this allows the educator to live on **$63,000 the first year after they stop working in a**

WRS-covered job, which is **90% of their highest average salary**. (Again, you can change any of those assumptions, including the final average salary and the percent of that you need to live on.) We assume that someone who wants to retire this early is comfortable living on a bit less and/or has adequately saved and invested in order to prepare for this moment. We've initially populated the spreadsheet with a starting balance of $0 in their investment account and then have them contribute $1,200 per month for the rest of their career. Since most of you are likely part way through your career, you can change those to whatever your current balance is, the number of years you have left in your career, and how much you are investing - or project you will invest - each month to match your situation.

They do not start drawing Social Security until age 67, so they need to withdraw from their investment account to make up the difference between their pension and what they need to live on. These withdrawals start at about 5.6% of their balance and increase to 6.3% of their balance by age 66. Withdrawals of this size each year are not sustainable over time, but they don't have to be, because once they start receiving Social Security, they will need to withdraw a much lower percentage (2% or less) from their investment accounts.

You'll also see that, based on the return assumption, the balance in their tax-advantaged investment account (403b/457/IRA) gets really large over time. But, again, note the information about **sequence of return risk** mentioned previously. If those larger drawdowns in those first years before Social Security kicks in are combined with poor market returns, the balance in the 403b could be dramatically lower (and even go to zero). Should you choose a scenario such as this one, you'll have to determine your comfort level with this scenario as we've laid it out and make adjustments as necessary (work longer, save/invest more, and/or spend less).

On the other hand, if you have a positive sequence of returns at the beginning of your retirement under this scenario, then your balance would increase as shown (or perhaps even more quickly), and you could then choose to withdraw - and spend - more than indicated in the spreadsheet. (Or, alternatively, you could start with a lower balance in your tax-advantaged account, but that does increase your exposure to sequence of return risk.) We think planning on a base spending level that you can live on makes sense and then, if the market does well, you can choose to increase your discretionary spending.

The bottom line for this scenario is that it is very possible for an educator to retire at age 60 with 20 years of experience if they make choices along the way that grows their investments. They need to **start investing as much as they can as early as they can, and increase that investment when they are able to**, and make realistic projections about how much they will have accumulated in their tax advantaged accounts by age 60. They also need to **make realistic assumptions about how much they will need to live on in retirement,** by avoiding lifestyle creep and being able to live on a bit less than they were earning at the end of their career (or have a much larger balance in their 403b account when they retire so that they can withdraw more to support their spending).

Scenario 4: Tier 2, Retire at Age 55, 30 Years of Service, Rule of 85

Our fourth scenario looks at a Tier 2 educator who wants to stop working at a WRS-covered job at **age 55 and has 30 years of service (so they get a full pension)**.

While you can **start drawing Social Security at age 62, it's advantageous to wait until age 67 (or 70)**, so this scenario relies on the educator filling the "gap" years between stopping working and drawing Social Security at age 67 by drawing down their tax-advantaged investment account(s). Once they start receiving Social Security, then the remaining balance in the investment account is tapped to help supplement their pension.

Here are the **assumptions** we've made for the base case for this scenario:

1. **Stop Working at a WRS-covered job**: Age 55
2. **Start Drawing Pension**: Age 55
3. **Years of Service**: 30
4. **Multiplier**: 60%
5. **Current Balance in tax-advantaged investment account (403b/457/IRA)**: $0
6. **Monthly Investment in tax-advantaged investment account (403b/457/IRA)**: $400 ($4,800/year)
7. **Years Remaining to Invest**: 30
8. **Annual Return on investments**: 7%
9. **Highest Average Salary**: $70,000
10. **Replacement Income**: 85% of Highest Average Salary
11. **Yearly Increase in Retirement Income**: 2% through age 65, 1% after age 65
12. **Social Security Replacement Percentage**: 37%
13. **Age Begin Drawing Social Security**: 67
14. **Annual Reduction in Benefit**: 0%

Visit **fischlearning.com/tldr-wyoming** and click on the link for Scenario 4 to see the spreadsheet that illustrates this scenario with the above assumptions. Remember, you can change any of the numbers in the **green shaded cells** if you want to change any of the assumptions.

As you can see from the spreadsheet, this allows the educator to live on **$59,500 the first year after they stop working in a WRS-covered job**, which is **85% of their highest average salary**. (Again, you can change any of those assumptions, including the final average salary and the percent of that you need to live on.) We assume that someone who wants to retire this early is comfortable living on a bit less and/or has adequately saved and invested in order to prepare for this moment. We've initially populated the spreadsheet with a starting balance of $0 in their investment account and then have them contribute $400 per month for the rest of their career. Since most of you are likely part way through your career, you can change those to whatever your current balance is, the number of years you have left in your career, and how much you are investing - or project you will invest - each month to match your situation.

They do not start drawing Social Security until age 67, so they need to withdraw from their investment account to make up the difference between their pension and what they need to live on. These withdrawals start at about 3.8% of their balance and increase to 5.51% of their balance by age 66. Withdrawals of this size each year are not sustainable over time, but they don't have to be, because once they start receiving Social Security, they will need to withdraw a much lower percentage (1% or less) from their investment accounts.

You'll also see that, based on the return assumption, the balance in their tax-advantaged investment account (403b/457/IRA) gets really large over time. But, again, note the information about **sequence of return risk** mentioned previously. If those larger drawdowns in those first years before Social Security kicks in are combined with poor market returns, the balance in the 403b could be dramatically lower (and even go to zero). Should you choose a scenario such as this one, you'll have to determine your comfort level with this scenario as we've laid it out and make adjustments as necessary (work longer, save/invest more, and/or spend less).

On the other hand, if you have a positive sequence of returns at the beginning of your retirement under this scenario, then your balance would increase as shown (or perhaps even more quickly), and you could then choose to withdraw - and spend - more than indicated in the spreadsheet. (Or, alternatively, you could start with a lower balance in your tax-advantaged account, but that does increase your exposure to sequence of return risk.) We think planning on a base spending level that you can live on makes sense and then, if the market does well, you can choose to increase your discretionary spending.

The bottom line for this scenario is that it is very possible for a Tier 2 educator to retire at age 55 with 30 years of experience if they make choices along the way that grows their investments. They need to start investing as much as they can as early as they can, and increase that investment when they are able to, and make realistic projections about how much they will have accumulated in their tax advantaged accounts by age 55. They also need to **make realistic assumptions about how much they will need to live on in retirement,** by avoiding lifestyle creep and being able to live on a bit less than they were earning at the end of their career (or have a much larger balance in their 403b account when they retire so that they can withdraw more to support their spending).

Scenario 5: Tier 2, Retire at Age 60, 23 Years of Service, Reduced Benefit

Our fifth scenario looks at a Tier 2 educator who wants to stop working at a WRS-covered job at **age 60 and has 23 years of service (so they will get a reduced pension).**

While you can **start drawing Social Security at age 62, it's advantageous to wait until age 67 (or 70),** so this scenario relies on the educator filling the "gap" years between stopping working and drawing Social Security at age 67 by drawing down their tax-advantaged investment account(s). Once they start receiving Social Security, then the remaining balance in the investment account is tapped to help supplement their pension.

Here are the **assumptions** we've made for the base case for this scenario:

1. **Stop Working at a WRS-covered job**: Age 60
2. **Start Drawing Pension**: Age 60

3. **Years of Service**: 23
4. **Multiplier**: 46%
5. **Current Balance in tax-advantaged investment account (403b/457/IRA)**: $0
6. **Monthly Investment in tax-advantaged investment account (403b/457/IRA)**: $1,200 ($14,400/year)
7. **Years Remaining to Invest**: 23
8. **Annual Return on investments**: 7%
9. **Highest Average Salary**: $70,000
10. **Replacement Income**: 80% of Highest Average Salary
11. **Yearly Increase in Retirement Income**: 2% through age 65, 1% after age 65
12. **Social Security Replacement Percentage**: 37%
13. **Age Begin Drawing Social Security**: 67
14. **Annual Reduction in Benefit**: 25%

Visit **fischlearning.com/tldr-wyoming** and click on the link for Scenario 5 to see the spreadsheet that illustrates this scenario with the above assumptions. Remember, you can change any of the numbers in the **green shaded cells** if you want to change any of the assumptions.

> **Note**: We have included this scenario as it may apply to some folks, but keep in mind that if they chose to work for just one more year, they would meet the Rule of 85 (they would be 61 with 24 years) and thereby avoid the 25% reduction in benefits. While there may be a compelling reason not to work that additional year, it makes a huge financial difference so consider carefully.

As you can see from the spreadsheet, this allows the educator to live on **$56,000 the first year after they stop working in a WRS-covered job**, which is **80% of their highest average salary**. (Again, you can change any of those assumptions, including the final average salary and the percent of that you need to live on.) We assume that someone who wants to retire at this age and years of service is comfortable living on a bit less and/or has adequately saved and invested in order to prepare for this moment. We've initially populated the spreadsheet with a starting balance of $0 in their investment account and then have them contribute $1,200 per month for the rest of their career. Since most of you are likely part way through your career, you can change those to whatever your current balance is, the number of years you have left in your career, and how much you are investing - or project you will invest - each month to match your situation.

They do not start drawing Social Security until age 67, so they need to withdraw from their investment account to make up the difference between their pension and what they need to live on. These withdrawals start at about 4.1% of their balance and increase to about 4.5% of their balance by age 66. Withdrawals of this size each year may not be sustainable over time, but they don't have to be, because once they start receiving Social Security, they will need to withdraw a much lower percentage (less than 2%) from their investment accounts.

You'll also see that, based on the return assumption, the balance in their tax-advantaged investment account (403b/457/IRA) gets really large over time. But, again, note the information about **sequence of return risk** mentioned previously. If those larger drawdowns in those first years before Social Security kicks in are combined with poor market returns, the balance in the 403b could be dramatically lower (and even go to zero). Should you choose a scenario such as this one, you'll have to determine your comfort level with this scenario as we've laid it out and make adjustments as necessary (work longer, save/invest more, and/or spend less).

On the other hand, if you have a positive sequence of returns at the beginning of your retirement under this scenario, then your balance would increase as shown (or perhaps even more quickly), and you could then choose to withdraw - and spend - more than indicated in the spreadsheet. (Or, alternatively, you could start with a lower balance in your tax-advantaged account, but that does increase your exposure to sequence of return risk.) We think planning on a base spending level that you can live on makes sense and then, if the market does well, you can choose to increase your discretionary spending.

The bottom line for this scenario is that it is very possible for a Tier 2 educator to retire at age 60 with 23 years of experience if they make choices along the way that grows their investments. **(Although, again, if at all possible working one more year would make a big difference.)** They need to start investing as much as they can as early as they can, and increase that investment when they are able to, and make realistic projections about how much they will have accumulated in their tax advantaged accounts by age 60. They also need to **make realistic assumptions about how much they will need to live on in retirement,** by avoiding lifestyle creep and being able to live on a bit less than they were earning at the end of their career (or have a much larger balance in their 403b account when they retire so that they can withdraw more to support their spending).

Scenario 6: Tier 2, Retire at Age 65, 35 Years of Service, Full Benefit

Our sixth scenario looks at a Tier 2 educator who wants to stop working at a WRS-covered job at **age 65 and has 35 years of service (so they will get a full pension).**

While you can **start drawing Social Security at age 62, it's advantageous to wait until age 67 (or 70),** so this scenario relies on the educator filling the "gap" years between stopping working and drawing Social Security at age 67 by drawing down their tax-advantaged investment account(s). Once they start receiving Social Security, then the remaining balance in the investment account is tapped to help supplement their pension.

Here are the **assumptions** we've made for the base case for this scenario:

1. **Stop Working at a WRS-covered job**: Age 65
2. **Start Drawing Pension**: Age 65
3. **Years of Service**: 35
4. **Multiplier**: 70%
5. **Current Balance in tax-advantaged investment account (403b/457/IRA)**: $0
6. **Monthly Investment in tax-advantaged investment account (403b/457/IRA)**: $200 ($2,400/year)
7. **Years Remaining to Invest**: 35
8. **Annual Return on investments**: 7%
9. **Highest Average Salary**: $70,000
10. **Replacement Income**: 90% of Highest Average Salary
11. **Yearly Increase in Retirement Income**: 2% through age 65, 1% after age 65
12. **Social Security Replacement Percentage**: 37%
13. **Age Begin Drawing Social Security**: 67
14. **Annual Reduction in Benefit**: 0%

Visit **fischlearning.com/tldr-wyoming** and click on the link for Scenario 6 to see the spreadsheet that illustrates this scenario with the above assumptions. Remember, you can change any of the numbers in the **green shaded cells** if you want to change any of the assumptions.

As you can see from the spreadsheet, this allows the educator to live on **$63,000 the first year after they stop working in a WRS-covered job**, which is **90% of their highest average salary**. (Again, you can change any of those assumptions, including the final average salary and the percent of that you need to live on.) We assume that someone who wants to retire at this age and years of service is comfortable living on a bit less and/or has adequately saved and invested in order to prepare for this moment. We've initially populated the spreadsheet with a starting balance of $0 in their investment account and then have them contribute $200 per month for the rest of their career. Since most of you are likely part way through your career, you can change those to whatever your current balance is, the number of years you have left in your career, and how much you are investing - or project you will invest - each month to match your situation.

They do not start drawing Social Security until age 67, so they need to withdraw from their investment account to make up the difference between their pension and what they need to live on. These withdrawals are a bit over 4% of their balance. Withdrawals of this size each year may not be sustainable over time, but they don't have to be, because once they start receiving Social Security, they will need to withdraw very little from their investment accounts.

You'll also see that, based on the return assumption, the balance in their tax-advantaged investment account (403b/457/IRA) gets really large over time. But, again, note the information about **sequence of return risk** mentioned previously. If those larger drawdowns in those first years before Social Security kicks in are combined with poor market returns, the balance in the 403b could be dramatically lower (and even go to zero). Should you choose a scenario such as this one, you'll have to determine your comfort level with this scenario as we've laid it out and make adjustments as necessary (work longer, save/invest more, and/or spend less).

On the other hand, if you have a positive sequence of returns at the beginning of your retirement under this scenario, then your balance would increase as shown (or perhaps even more quickly), and you could then choose to withdraw - and spend - more than indicated in the spreadsheet. (Or, alternatively, you could start with a lower balance in your tax-advantaged account, but that does increase your exposure to sequence of return risk.) We think planning on a base spending level that you can live on makes sense and then, if the market does well, you can choose to increase your discretionary spending.

The bottom line for this scenario is that it is very possible for a

Tier 2 educator to retire at age 65 with 35 years of experience if they make choices along the way that grows their investments. They need to start investing as much as they can as early as they can, and increase that investment when they are able to, and make realistic projections about how much they will have accumulated in their tax advantaged accounts by age 65. They also need to **make realistic assumptions about how much they will need to live on in retirement,** by avoiding lifestyle creep and being able to live on a bit less than they were earning at the end of their career (or have a much larger balance in their 403b account when they retire so that they can withdraw more to support their spending).

CONCLUSION: SUSTAINABILITY

TL;DR: Sustainability is about more than just the environment, it's about designing your life in such a way that you can live the "good life" you want to live.

"Often when you think you're at the end of something, you're at the beginning of something else."— Fred Rogers

The idea of sustainability is most often associated with the environment, but it also applies to your financial life. The whole purpose of this book is to help you get started on a path that allows you to live your best life, the life you want to lead. Inherent in that is the idea of sustainability, the ability to sustain the life that you want to lead.

Hopefully the **very brief introduction** that this book provided to some of the important financial decisions you need to make will get you interested enough to learn more about these issues. You don't have to be an accountant, a Wall Street trader, or a tax expert to make good decisions, you just need a little bit of knowledge and the wisdom to act on that knowledge.

Just a reminder that this was designed for the TL;DR reader, so it didn't explain the reasons why to do each thing or link to the data that backs each assertion ("about 100 pages, about an hour or two"). We even recommended in the introduction that you probably shouldn't buy or read this book, that instead you should spend some time exploring more thorough and in-depth resources. So, while this book gives you a good start and you hopefully found it helpful, if it's sparked your curiosity and you're willing to invest a bit more time to learn more you will achieve even better results. There are many, many, many resources (books, websites, online communities, etc.) available to you, we've tried to curate just a few of them at **fischlearning.com/tldr-wyoming**. Good luck making the financial decisions that will help you lead **your good life.**

◆ ◆ ◆

If you liked this book and found it helpful, please consider leaving a rating or review on Amazon. Please also consider recommending it (or loaning it!) to other Wyoming public school employees. If you are an administrator, superintendent, school board member, or union leader, consider purchasing this book for your new teachers each year. It not only will make a difference in their financial lives, but it will allow them to be even better teachers because they feel confident in their finances.

If you have questions or feedback, or simply want to talk about your financial situation, please reach out to us at **karl@fischlearning.com** or **jillkthompson@gmail.com** and/or leave feedback at **bit.ly/tldrfeedback** (really, we *like* talking about this stuff).

Learn More

fischlearning.com/tldr/

fischlearning.com/tldr_resources/

fischlearning.com/tldr-wyoming/

Twitter: @karlfisch and @jillkthompson

Facebook: facebook.com/karlfisch/

TL;DR: GETTING STARTED

Spend less than you make and invest the rest in low-cost, diversified index funds with an asset allocation appropriate for your risk tolerance and investment time horizon.

1. **Bank Accounts and Credit Cards (1.5 & 1.6):** Optimize these and choose the best accounts for your circumstances.

2. **Income (1.14 & 3.1):** Advance horizontally on the salary schedule as far as you can as quickly as you can.

3. **Investments (1.10-1.13 & 3.2):** For **all** of your investments (401k, 403b, 457, IRA, HSA, Taxable Brokerage Account), make sure you are not with a high-fee vendor or have high-fee investments. If you do, switch to a low-fee vendor and invest in low-cost, diversified index funds. Also think carefully about both your asset allocation and your risk tolerance and perhaps make adjustments.

4. **Pension (All of Part 2 & 3.1):** Take the time to figure out if you are eligible to purchase service credit and seriously consider doing that if you are eligible. Also consider earning extra income during your HAS years.

5. **Retirement Scenarios (4.2):** Take some time to play around with some of the retirement scenarios just to familiarize yourself with the possibilities. Think carefully about how your pension (WRS) and additional investments (401k/403b/457/IRA/Taxable Brokerage) can add up to help you live your 'good life' in retirement.

Learn More: Visit **fischlearning.com/tldr_resources/** and **fischlearning.com/tldr-wyoming/** and explore the resources available there to continue your financial education.

Made in the USA
Coppell, TX
17 March 2023

14384278R00066